Collins

AS Revision**Notes**
Psychology

Mike Cardwell • Jane Willson

Series editor: Jayne de Courcy

William Collins' dream of knowledge for all began with the publication of his first book in 1819. A self-educated mill worker, he not only enriched millions of lives, but also founded a flourishing publishing house. Today, staying true to this spirit, Collins books are packed with inspiration, innovation and practical expertise. They place you at the centre of a world of possibility and give you exactly what you need to explore it.

Collins. Do more.

Published by Collins
An imprint of HarperCollinsPublishers
77 – 85 Fulham Palace Road
Hammersmith
London
W6 8JB

Browse the complete Collins catalogue at
www.collinseducation.com

© HarperCollinsPublishers Limited 2006

10 9 8 7 6 5 4 3 2 1

ISBN-13 978 0 00 720695 7
ISBN-10 0 00 720695 X

Mike Cardwell and Jane Willson assert the moral right to be identified as the authors of this work

British Library Cataloguing in Publication Data
A Catalogue record for this publication is available from the British Library

Edited by Jenny Draine
Production by Katie Butler
Series and book design by Sally Boothroyd
Artwork by Jerry Fowler
Index compiled by Joan Dearnley
Printed and bound by Printing Express, Hong Kong

You might also like to visit
www.harpercollins.co.uk
The book lover's website

CONTENTS

HOW THIS BOOK WILL HELP YOU

This book has been designed to make your revision as easy and effective as possible.

Here's how:

SHORT, ACCESSIBLE NOTES THAT YOU CAN INTEGRATE INTO YOUR REVISION FILE

Collins Revision Notes AS Psychology have been prepared by top examiners who know exactly what you need to revise in order to be successful.

You can *either* base your revision on this book *or* you can tear off the notes and integrate them into your own revision file. This will ensure that you have the best possible notes to revise from.

STUDENT-FRIENDLY PRESENTATION

The notes use visual aids – flowcharts, tables, boxes, etc. – so the content is easier to remember.

There is also systematic use of colour to help you revise:

MUST KNOW...
Green panels summarise what you need to revise.

MUST REMEMBER ...
Red panels panels draw attention to key aspects.

MUST TAKE CARE...
Purple panels highlight tricky areas.

Dark blue outline and tint panels contain research studies.

Orange outline and tint panels indicate AO2 commentary and evaluation.

Green outline *panels contain short hints for using the information in exam questions.*

Yellow highlighting or **bold** emphasise important words and phrases.

CONTENT MATCHED TO YOUR SPECIFICATION

This book has primarily been designed to cover the AQA AS Psychology specification. If you are following the OCR AS Psychology specification, you will still find it useful to revise from this book and its companion, *Collins Revision Notes A2 Psychology*.

GUIDANCE ON EXAM TECHNIQUE

This book concentrates on providing you with the best possible revision notes.

At the end of each unit there are also some typical questions, with hints, so that you can see how you will need to apply your knowledge. If you want more guidance on exam technique, then use *Collins Exam Practice AS Psychology* in conjunction with these Revision Notes.

Using both these books will help you to achieve a high grade in your AS Psychology exams.

SHORT-TERM AND LONG-TERM MEMORY

MUST KNOW...
- Research into the nature of STM and LTM.

DEFINITION

Memory: mental processes involved in registering, storing and retrieving information.

STM: limited capacity system for storing information for short periods.

LTM: unlimited capacity system for storing information for long periods.

MUST TAKE CARE...
Not to confuse STM and LTM.

MUST REMEMBER...
That STM and LTM operate differently.

WHAT ARE THE DIFFERENCES?

	STM	LTM
Capacity (the amount of information that can be stored at any one time)	Very limited.	Unlimited.
Duration (the length of time information can be stored)	Very short without rehearsal.	A few seconds to almost a lifetime.
Encoding (how information is changed into a form that can be stored)	Mainly acoustic (preferred code).	Mainly semantic (preferred code).

OUTLINE OF RESEARCH FINDINGS INTO THE NATURE OF STM

FINDINGS

Capacity

- 7 +/−2 (Miller, 1956).
- Digit span improved by:
  – chunking
  – reading aloud
  – practice
  – rhythmic grouping.
- Limited by pronunciation time (Baddeley et al., 1975).

Duration

- Rehearsal required to maintain material in STM.
- Rapid loss of information when rehearsal is prevented.
- Memory for words is longer-lasting than memory for isolated letters.

Encoding

- More difficult to recall strings of acoustically similar letters than visually similar ones (Conrad, 1964).
- More difficult to recall similar sounding words to words of similar meaning (Baddeley).

Criticisms can be positive as well as negative.

CRITICISMS

Capacity

- Research based on artificial laboratory experiments.
- Difficult to exclude influence of LTM.

Duration

- Research frequently based on artificial stimulus material such as trigrams – might not reflect everyday memory.
- Findings might reflect instructions given to participants, e.g. duration improves when there is a conscious effort to recall.

Encoding

- Research is mainly based on artificial laboratory experiments.
- Acoustic coding seems to be preferred method of coding but not the only one. If acoustic coding is prevented, visual coding is possible (Brandimonte et al., 1992).

OUTLINE OF RESEARCH FINDINGS INTO THE NATURE OF LTM

FINDINGS

Duration

- LTM can last almost a lifetime.
- Thorough initial learning of material increases duration of storage.

Encoding

- Semantically similar words are harder to recall then semantically dissimilar words, and harder than acoustically similar and acoustically dissimilar words (Baddeley, 1966).

CRITICISMS

Duration

- It is difficult to test LTM duration because of the problem of controlling extraneous variables.
- The method of measuring recall can affect estimates of the length of duration, i.e. people remember information from long ago better if tested by recognition rather than recall.

Encoding

- Research is mainly based on artificial laboratory experiments.
- In everyday life, we instantly recognise certain sounds, e.g. phones ringing, suggesting that we can code acoustically in LTM.

MUST REMEMBER...
One study in detail (APFCC) on the nature of STM and **one** on the nature of LTM.

APFCC STUDIES ON THE NATURE OF STM AND LTM

	STM (Peterson and Peterson, 1959)	LTM (Bahrick et al., 1975)
A	To see how long STM lasts without rehearsal.	To test the duration of LTM using recognition and recall.
P	• Gave participants consonant trigram, e.g. GKX. Asked participants to count backwards in 3s. • Asked participants to recall trigrams after interval (3, 6, 9, 12, 15 or 18 seconds). • Gave participants several trials using different trigrams and different intervals.	• Tracked down graduates from an American High School who have left in the last 50 years. • **Recognition group:** asked them to match photos to a list of names. • **Recall group:** showed them photos from their high-school year book and asked them to name the people in the photos (NB no list provided).
F	• Participants able to recall 80% after 3 seconds. • Recall declined rapidly, the longer the interval. • After 18 seconds, fewer than 10% recalled.	• **Recognition group:** 90% correct after 14 years graduation, 80% after 25 years, 75% after 34 years and 60% after 47 years. • **Recall group:** 60% correct after 7 years and less than 20% after 47 years.
C	• Information disappears very rapidly if rehearsal is prevented. • Forgetting in STM is due to decay.	• People can remember certain types of information for almost a lifetime. • The accuracy of very long-term memory is better when tested by recognition than by recall.
C	• Laboratory experiment – artificial stimuli – not like real life. • Another interpretation possible, e.g. interference from previous trigrams inhibits recall.	• Tested people on real-life memories (positive criticism). • No real control on what participants had been doing in the interim (e.g. how often they looked at their year books or met old high-school peers). • Not clear whether drop-off in accuracy reflects limits of duration or a more general decline in memory with age.

TYPICAL QUESTIONS...

AO1 QUESTIONS

1 What is meant by the terms 'STM' and 'LTM'? (3 + 3 marks)

2 Describe the procedures and findings of one study into the nature of STM. (6 marks) *Any of PFCC could be chosen for this kind of question.*

3 Describe the procedures of one study into the nature of STM and give one criticism of this study. (3 + 3 marks)

4 Describe the conclusions of one study into the nature of LTM and give one criticism of this study. (3 + 3 marks)

5 Outline two differences between STM and LTM. (3 + 3 marks)

6 Outline findings of research into the nature into LTM. (6 marks)

AO1 + AO2 QUESTIONS

7 Outline and evaluate research into the nature of STM. (18 marks)

8 Outline and evaluate research into the nature of LTM. (18 marks)

THE MULTI-STORE MODEL OF MEMORY (ATKINSON AND SHIFFRIN)

MUST KNOW...
- How the model works.
- Research related to the model and the strengths and weaknesses of the model.

MUST REMEMBER...
That a model is an **explanation** or **theory** and is not the same as a study. A **study** is an investigation carried out to support or challenge the model.

MUST TAKE CARE...
That an outline of the multi-store model (MSM) includes a mention of processes (i.e. rehearsal, attention, re-coding) as well as an account of the stores and their characteristics.

THE MSM (brief outline)

- Is a **structural** model.
- Contains **three separate stores** (sensory, short-term and long-term).
- Sensory store is made up of **five stores**: one for each of the **senses**.
- STM and LTM are **unitary**, i.e. each store is a single unit with no divisions.
- Information passes from store to store in a fixed sequence (**linear**).
- **Attention** is needed to pass information on from sensory memory.
- **Rehearsal** is needed to pass information from STM to LTM.
- Each store has its own characteristics in terms of encoding, capacity and duration.
- Transfer between stages often requires re-coding.
- Information can be lost from each store.

HOW IT WORKS

For practice in answering AS Psychology questions, why not use *Collins Exam Practice AS Psychology*?

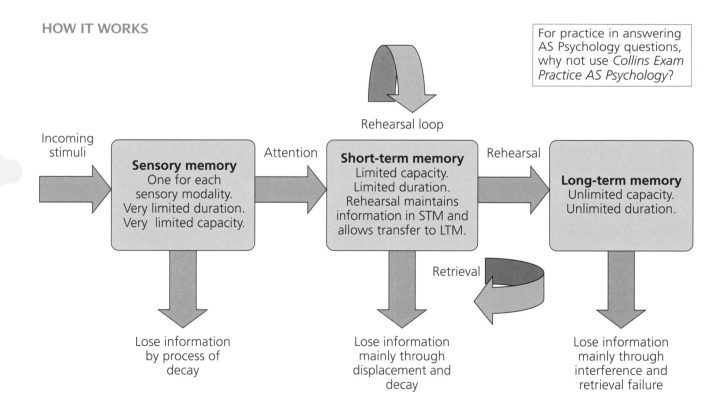

Rehearsal loop

Incoming stimuli → **Sensory memory** One for each sensory modality. Very limited duration. Very limited capacity.

Attention →

Short-term memory Limited capacity. Limited duration. Rehearsal maintains information in STM and allows transfer to LTM.

Rehearsal →

Long-term memory Unlimited capacity. Unlimited duration.

Retrieval

Lose information by process of decay

Lose information mainly through displacement and decay

Lose information mainly through interference and retrieval failure

EVALUATION OF THE MULTI-STORE MODEL

STRENGTHS

- Influential pioneering research that has stimulated important further study.
- Concept of a distinction between STM and LTM has been revised, but provides a useful framework for describing and understanding memory.
- Considerable body of research supports the idea of separate stores.

- Peterson and Peterson found that the duration of STM is severely limited in the absence of rehearsal, whereas Bahrick et al. found that LTM memories can last almost a lifetime.

- **Clinical evidence:**
  - Milner (1966) studied HM who had normal STM digit span but could not lay down new memories in LTM.
  - Clive Wearing (reported by Baddeley) also has problems transferring new items from STM to LTM.
- Research from PET and MRI scans has shown that different parts of the brain are activated depending on whether individuals are working on a LTM or STM task (Squire, 1992).

- Baddeley found evidence that STM encodes acoustically, and LTM codes semantically.

- Glanzer and Cunitz (1966) found evidence for primacy and recency effects in a free recall task – this suggests that early items are rehearsed sufficiently to transfer to LTM and most recent items are still circulating in STM. This study also supports the role of rehearsal in transferring information from STM to LTM.

WHAT QUESTIONS DOES THE MODEL RAISE?

- Are STM and LTM unitary?
- Is the passage of information linear?
- Is rehearsal a vital process?
- Can human memory be explained so simply?

- Baddeley has found evidence to support working memory model that STM is divided into separate components.
- Tulving (1968) has found that there are different types of LTM.

- Chunking in STM is only possible if LTM influences STM. Visual information, e.g. 'M' can only be recoded acoustically for STM if LTM provides information about letter shapes and sounds.

- Shallice found that KF could pass information to LTM even though his STM was grossly impaired.
- Craik and Lockhart (1972) found that simple maintenance rehearsal was not particularly important – what determines storage in LTM is depth of processing.
- Eysenck and Keane (1995) have suggested that information is constantly entering LTM without conscious rehearsal.

- Memory is probably much more complex and flexible than the MSM suggests. For example, MSM emphasises the amount of information to be processed, whereas the nature of the information may be the important factor, i.e. some things are simply easier to recall than others. MSM cannot account for this.

TYPICAL QUESTIONS...

AO1 QUESTIONS

1 Describe **any one** model of memory. (6 marks)

Model of memory = multi-store, working memory or levels of processing model. NB Must not confuse with 'study'.

2 Describe the multi-store model of memory. (6 marks)

3 Outline the multi-store model of memory and give one criticism of the model. (3 + 3 marks)

Look at the mark allocation – 'outline' requires less detail than 'describe'. Remember that criticisms can be positive as well as negative.

4 Give two criticisms of the multi-store model of memory. (3 + 3 marks)

AO1 + AO2 QUESTIONS

5 Outline and evaluate the multi-store model of memory. (18 marks)

6 'The multi-store model of memory has helped us to understand how memory works but may now have outlived its usefulness.' Outline the multi-store model of memory and consider its strengths **and/or** limitations. (18 marks)

Remember that AO1 marks = 6. Must not write more than would do for an AO1 question. AO2 marks = 12 (i.e. two thirds of essay). Try to include strengths and weaknesses.

The quotation is there to help – must not write it out and do not need to refer to it. Focus is on the actual question. Remember the AO1/AO2 split – two thirds of the answer should be evaluation.

ALTERNATIVES TO THE MULTI-STORE MODEL (I)

THE WORKING MEMORY MODEL
(BADDELEY AND HITCH)

MUST KNOW...
- How the model works.
- Research related to the model and the strengths and weaknesses of the model.

THE WORKING MEMORY MODEL (brief outline)
- Is a functional model (i.e. explains how the memory works).
- Focuses on the STM component of memory.
- Contains separate components, i.e. is *not* unitary.
- Each component specialises in particular tasks.
- The components do not simply store information – they also manipulate and analyse the information.
- Central executive is the controlling component and acts like an attentional system.
- Central executive supervises and coordinates subsidiary systems called 'slave systems'.
- Visuo-spatial scratch pad deals with visual images.
- Phonological loop deals with auditory information and is sub-divided into the phonological store and the articulatory control system.
- Phonological store acts as inner ear whereas articulatory control system acts as inner voice.
- There is a two-way flow of information between the central executive and its slave systems.
- Explains how we can do two tasks simultaneously provided they use different modalities (i.e. one is visual and one is auditory).

HOW IT WORKS

Central executive
- Most important component.
- Monitor and coordinator of system.
- Flexible – can process information from any modality.
- Very limited storage capacity.
- Synthesises information from slave systems and LTM.

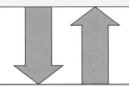

Phonological loop

Visuo-spatial scratchpad
- Acts as inner eye.
- Stores visual/spatial information briefly.
- Displays and manipulates visual/spatial information.
- Limited capacity.

Phonological store
- Inner ear
- Holds spoken words (written words have to be recorded).
- Limited capacity (amount that can be articulated in approximately two seconds).

Articulatory control system
- Inner voice
- Rehearses information from phonological store.
- Circulates information like a tape loop.
- Converts written material into articulatory code.

EVALUATION OF THE WORKING MEMORY MODEL

- Can explain how we manage a range of tasks, e.g. reading, verbal reasoning, visual and spatial processing.
- Can explain how we can carry out more than one cognitive task simultaneously provided we use different components.

STRENGTHS

- Recognises that STM must be made up of more than one component.
- Has greater explanatory power than the MSM.
- Removes the emphasis on rehearsal as a vital process.
- Is supported by a large body of experimental evidence.

- Emphasis on rehearsal is a weakness of the MSM because in life we do not always rehearse information and yet manage to remember much of it. In WM, rehearsal *only* takes place in the phonological loop.

USEFUL EXAMPLES OF SUPPORTING RESEARCH	
Findings	Conclusions
• Baddeley and Hitch (1974) found that participants could rehearse digit strings while completing verbal reasoning tasks.	• Participants can complete two different cognitive tasks simultaneously – this shows that STM must consist of more than one component.
• Baddeley et al. (1975) found that participants can recall more short words than long in an immediate serial recall task (word length effect).	• Short words take less time to articulate than long words – shows that the phonological loop must have a time-based capacity.
• Baddeley et al. (1975) found that the word length effect disappears if the phonological loop is filled with irrelevant information e.g. 'la...la...la'.	• Some words were still recalled even though there was no difference between short and long – suggests that the central executive might take over the task when necessary but is not as efficient as the specialised slave system.
• Baddeley et al. (1974) found that participants could not simultaneously carry out a tracking task and count the angles in an imagined figure.	• Tasks that require visual and/or spatial processing cannot be done simultaneously – suggests they are both competing for the limited capacity in the visuo-spatial scratch pad.
• Shallice and Warrington (1970) studied KF who had sustained brain damage in an accident. He had grossly impaired STM for verbal information, but could recall and manipulate visual information normally.	• Verbal and visual information are handled independently in STM. The MSM cannot explain this, but WM can.

- The idea of a central control mechanism makes sense, but the WM does not explain exactly how it works. For example, how does it decide which tasks need to be allocated? How does it coordinate information from the slave systems? We know that the central executive has a limited capacity, but no-one has yet been able to quantify this experimentally. Given that this is the most important part of the WM, it is a weakness of the model that so little is known about how it works.

WHAT QUESTIONS DOES THE MODEL RAISE?

- How does the central executive work?
- Is the model falsifiable?
- What happend so information that cannot be coded visually or acoustically or could be coded in both modalities?

- Critics (e.g. Richardson, 1984) suggest that the model can be used to explain any results, i.e. it gives rise to circular arguments. For example, if we can do two cognitive tasks at the same time, we assume they are being carried out by separate components, but if we cannot, we assume they tap into the same component. This makes it difficult to falsify the model and, therefore, slightly undermines its validity.

- It is not clear how the slave systems are coordinated so we do not know how information that could be coded in both slave systems is put together, e.g. where a voice is coming from. It has also not been explained how we deal with information from the other senses, e.g. the memory of a touch or a smell.

ALTERNATIVES TO THE MULTI-STORE MODEL (2)

THE LEVELS OF PROCESSING MODEL
(CRAIK AND LOCKHART)

MUST REMEMBER...
That only need to know one alternative to MSM.

MUST KNOW...
- How the model works.
- Research related to the model and the strengths and weaknesses of the model.

THE LEVELS OF PROCESSING MODEL (brief outline)

- Does not entirely reject notion of separate stores but focuses on **processing** of information rather than on how it is stored.
- **Primary memory** is where information is re-circulated (maintenance rehearsal).
- Primary memory holds information just long enough to use it (e.g. looking up a phone number and holding it for long enough to dial it).
- Long-term retention requires more than simple maintenance rehearsal.
- Memory is an automatic **by-product of attention** (i.e. you do not have to learn material deliberately in order to remember it).
- Information can be encoded and processed **at different levels** – from shallow to deep. The deeper the processing, the stronger the memory.
- Depth is achieved through reasonably complex interaction with the stimulus, e.g. semantic processing, organisation, etc.

HOW IT WORKS

Experimental technique: show participants a word and a question printed on a card. Later, give them an unexpected recall test. They remember best the words they processed most deeply.

Example
You see the word:

DOG

SHALLOW LEVEL PROCESSING

Physical appearance (structural)
- What does the word look like?
- Do you recognise the shapes of the letters?
- Is it in capitals or lower case?

DEEPER LEVEL PROCESSING

Sound (acoustic)
- What does the word sound like when you say it?
- Does it rhyme with 'log'?
- Does it rhyme with 'cat'?

DEEPEST LEVEL PROCESSING

Meaning (semantic)
- What does the word mean?
- Is it an animal?
- Is it something you can eat?

EVALUATION OF THE LEVELS OF PROCESSING MODEL

STRENGTHS

- Influential approach.
- Explains why we remember certain things without rehearsal.
- Is supported by research studies.

- Welcomed as a refinement of MSM.
- Showed that encoding was not the simple process described in the MSM.

- We do not have to deliberately set out to remember things as long as we pay them attention. This could explain why we remember, e.g. flashbulb memories without obvious rehearsal.

- e.g. Hyde and Jenkins (1973) gave participants a list of words and asked them to answer various questions about them. They found no differences in recall between participants who had been instructed to recall the words and participants who had not. (This supports LOP because retention is a by-product of attention). They also found that recall was better for the words that had been analysed semantically, i.e. more deeply processed than for words which had simply been processed for appearance or sound.

WHAT QUESTIONS DOES THE MODEL RAISE?

- What is meant by 'depth'?
- Is the model falsifiable?
- Have research findings been misleading?

- The idea of depth is rather vague and poorly defined.
- There is no independent definition of what is meant by depth.
- Later studies suggested that depth could include factors such as elaboration, distinctiveness and effort.

- The model is descriptive rather than explanatory and also circulatory. If something is easily recalled, it is assumed that it was processed deeply and, if it is not well recalled, it is assumed it was processed shallowly. However, in the Hyde and Jenkins study, the task that gave rise to the lowest level of recall was deciding if a word fitted a particular sentence structure. This was assumed to be due to shallow processing. However, judgements about sentence frames would appear to require semantic analysis and, therefore, deep processing.

- There is some evidence to suggest that the method of recall demanded in the experiment is important. For example, in recognition tests, structural encoding can provide better recall than semantic encoding.

TYPICAL QUESTIONS...

AO1 QUESTIONS

1 Describe any **one** alternative model to the multi-store model of memory. (6 marks)

2 Outline **one** alternative to the multi-store model of memory and give **one** criticism of the model. (3 + 3 marks)

3 Choose any **one** alternative to the multi-store model of memory and give **two** criticisms of this model. (3 + 3 marks)

*Alternative model = working memory or LOP. Must not confuse with **study**.*

*'Outline' requires a bit less detail than 'describe'. Only **one** criticism required. Criticisms can be positive **or** negative.*

Only criticisms (positive and/or negative) required here. Must not waste time describing the model.

AO1 + AO2 QUESTIONS

4 Outline and evaluate any one alternative to the multi-store model of memory. (18 marks)

5 'The multi-store model has outlived its usefulness. Other models have proved more helpful in explaining memory process.' Outline any **one** alternative to the multi-store model of memory and consider its strengths and weaknesses in comparison to the multi-store model. (18 marks)

AO1 marks = 6. Must not write more than for an AO1 question.

AO2 = 12 marks (i.e. two thirds of essay). Must try to include strengths and weaknesses.

REMEMBERING AND FORGETTING (I)

MUST KNOW...
• Why we forget –
explanations of forgetting
in STM **and** LTM and
relevant research.

DEFINITION
Forgetting is the inability to recall or recognise something that has previously been learned.

EXPANSION
• This could be a problem of availability: the memory has disappeared completely from the memory store (usually STM).
• It could be a problem of accessibility: the memory is stored somewhere but is obscured in some way so that it cannot be found at that moment (usually LTM).

STM FORGETTING

Two main explanations DECAY

DISPLACEMENT

MUST TAKE CARE...
Not to explain a term by using the same word. Use words like 'push out' or 'make room for' instead of 'displace'.

	DECAY	DISPLACEMENT
Explanation	Based on the idea that a structural change occurs in the brain when a memory is laid down (Hebb, 1949). The memory trace is very fragile at first and easily disrupted. With rehearsal, the trace is strengthened and able to transfer to LTM. Without rehearsal, the trace remains fragile and disappears completely after a short time.	Based on the idea that STM has a very limited capacity (Miller, 1956). Material currently circulating in STM which has not yet been processed enough to go into LTM will be pushed out (displaced) by incoming, new information.
Research support	Reitman (1974): • Showed participants lists of five words for two seconds. • Gave a task that prevented rehearsal but did not interfere with learning (listening out to detect a tone for 15 seconds). • Recall declined by about 24% over the 15 second delay. • Interpolated task required effort and attention (so prevented rehearsal) but not new learning (so prevented displacement) – suggests the words had been forgotten because of decay.	Waugh and Norman (1965): • Used serial probe technique. • Presented 16 digits. Repeated one digit (probe). • Asked participants to recall digit that followed probe. • Participants could recall well if probe was near end of list but badly if probe was near beginning. • Suggests early digits had been displaced by later ones.

EVALUATION OF DECAY AND DISPLACEMENT

It is difficult to prevent rehearsal without introducing new information that could displace the original stimulus material.

It is difficult to disentangle the effects of decay from those of displacement.

MUST REMEMBER...
Could use either of these in an AO1 question that asks for one criticism of the explanation.

- **Peterson and Peterson** showed rapid forgetting of consonant trigrams and concluded that this was due to decay. However, there are other interpretations: displacement (i.e. the numbers in the interpolated counting task pushed out the trigrams) or proactive interference (i.e. the previous trigrams interfered with the ones presented later).

- **Reitman** tried to avoid these problems but could not be sure that no new information entered STM during the 15-second delay, i.e. she could not rule out displacement.

- **Shallice** repeated his serial probe technique experiment but varied the rate of presentation, i.e. he read out the digits either slowly or quickly. He found that participants were able to recall the probes at the beginning of the list better when presentation was at the rate of one word every one second than at the rate of one word every four seconds. This suggests that decay must be a factor in STM forgetting since displacement should not be affected by the time taken to read the list. However, he found that moving the position of the serial probe had a greater effect on forgetting than speeding up the presentation of the digits so concluded that displacement was the more important method of forgetting in STM.

SO, IS IT DECAY OR DISPLACEMENT? →

It is difficult to devise an experiment that disentangles the effects of decay and displacement. It is likely that forgetting in STM occurs through both these mechanisms, and that even interference might play a part.

For practice in answering AS Psychology questions, why not use *Collins Exam Practice AS Psychology*?

REMEMBERING AND FORGETTING (2)

LTM FORGETTING

Two main explanations

→ INTERFERENCE

↘ RETRIEVAL FAILURE

- **Trace decay** is also possible – thought to be the result of brain damage or the ageing process.

e.g. Tip-of the-tongue effect: you know the word is stored in LTM and can recognise it as soon as you are told it, but it is not readily accessible, so you cannot immediately retrieve it.

	INTERFERENCE	RETRIEVAL FAILURE
Explanation	One memory gets in the way of another memory and so gives rise to forgetting. There are *two* types of interference: - Retroactive: new information interferes with old. - Proactive: an old memory trace interferes with new information.	Information that has been learned cannot be accessed successfully. It is sometimes called cue-dependent forgetting because appropriate cues can sometimes be used to retrieve the memory.

Research support	- McGeoch and MacDonald (1931) asked participants to learn and re-learn lists of words and gave unrelated tasks in the interval.
	  – Forgetting was lowest when participants simply rested between learning and recall.
	  – Forgetting was highest when the interval task involved learning similar material.
	  – Suggests that retroactive interference is a factor in LTM forgetting and that it occurs most with similar material.
	- Underwood (1957) found evidence for proactive interference – students in his studies were less successful at learning new lists of words if they had learned many lists previously.
		- Tulving and Osler (1968) gave participants lists of weakly paired associate words, e.g. city – dirty. Participants then given either free recall or cued recall test.
		  – Cued recall produced better results than free recall.
		  – Suggests that memories that seem to be forgotten can sometimes be retrieved with the appropriate cue.
		- Smith (1970) found evidence that environment can act as a cue. Participants tested in the same room where they had learnt words recalled more than participants tested in a different room.
		- Goodwin et al. (1969) found that heavy drinkers, who learn things when drunk, recall them better when they are drunk again.

EVALUATION OF INTERFERENCE AND RETRIEVAL FAILURE

INTERFERENCE

- Much of the research investigating interference is laboratory-based using artificial stimuli – might not reflect how we forget in real life.

- There seems to be evidence that interference can cause forgetting particularly where the interfering material is very similar to the original material. However, studies by researchers like **Tulving** suggest that the problems occur at the retrieval rather than the learning stage.

- **Baddeley and Hitch** tried to carry out some ecologically valid research. Asked rugby players to recall the teams they had played in the last season. Results showed that forgetting was due to interference, i.e. number of games played, rather than simply to the time lapse.

RETRIEVAL FAILURE

- This seems to be one of the most convincing explanations and certain psychologists, e.g. **Eysenck (1998)**, believe that it is the main mechanism for forgetting in LTM.

- There is a lot of research that supports this explanation. Although the research is mainly laboratory-based, and therefore might not be representative, there is support from everyday experience. For example, forgetting details about your first school only to find the memories come flooding back if you visit the place again, or taking up a foreign language that you have not studied for years and finding that it is much easier to learn second time around.

MUST REMEMBER...
Could use any of these evaluative points in an AO1 question that asks for **one** criticism of the explanation.

MUST TAKE CARE...
To read the question carefully – make sure to notice whether the question is asking for STM or LTM.

For practice in answering AS Psychology questions, why not use *Collins Exam Practice AS Psychology*?

TYPICAL QUESTIONS...

AO1 QUESTIONS

1 Outline **one** explanation for forgetting in STM and **one** explanation for forgetting in LTM. (3 + 3 marks)

Make it clear to the examiner which explanation is for STM and which is for LTM.

2 Outline **one** explanation of forgetting in STM and give **one** criticism of this explanation. (3 + 3 marks)

Criticisms can be positive or negative.

3 Outline **two** explanations of forgetting in LTM. (3 + 3 marks)

AO1 + AO2 QUESTIONS

4 Outline and evaluate **one or more** explanations of forgetting in STM. (18 marks)

Must remember the depth/breadth trade-off. Lots of detail on one explanation, but less detail required if writing about two.

5 Outline and evaluate **two** explanations of forgetting in STM **or** LTM. (18 marks)

When question says 'or' – need to choose explanations from either STM or LTM – must not mix them up!

6 'Considering the huge amount of information we have to process throughout our lives, it is not surprising that we cannot remember everything.' Discuss research that helps us to understand forgetting in LTM. (18 marks)

THE ROLE OF EMOTIONAL FACTORS IN MEMORY

FLASHBULB MEMORIES (FBs)

DEFINITION

A flashbulb memory is a vivid, long-lasting memory associated with a highly significant event. We remember details about the context of the event such as where we were, when we heard the news and what we were doing at the time.

It's sometimes useful to include examples:
- the attack on the World Trade Centre (2001)
- the death of Princess Diana (1997)
- the death of the Pope (2005)
- the Asian Tsunami (2004).

EXPANSION

- Usually the event:
  - is highly significant
  - is emotional
  - is unexpected/surprising
  - has real consequences for the person who remembers, but can have personal significance (e.g. death of someone close) or have a wider impact (e.g. the attack on the World Trade Centre).
- Brown and Kulik (1977) were the first to describe this kind of memory. They believed that the emotion associated with the event triggers a neural mechanism that imprints the details on the memory – a bit like a photo. They found that the structural form of the memory was very similar regardless of the person remembering or the specific event. People tend to recall six types of information about the moment they heard the news:
  - where they were
  - what they were doing
  - the person who gave them the news
  - what they felt about it
  - what others felt about it
  - what happened in the immediate aftermath.

OUTLINE OF RESEARCH FINDINGS INTO FLASHBULB MEMORIES

RESEARCH IN SUPPORT OF FLASHBULB MEMORIES
Brown and Kulik (1977) asked black and white Americans to recall circumstances surrounding 10 momentous events:
- Almost all participants had FBs about the assassination of J.F. Kennedy.
- Participants tended to have greater recall of events related to someone of their own ethnic background, e.g. more black people had FBs for the death of Martin Luther King.
- Suggests that unexpectedness/shock is an important factor in FBs. The race effect confirms that personal significance is also an important factor.

RESEARCH AGAINST FLASHBULB MEMORIES
McCloskey et al. (1988) asked people about their memories surrounding the Challenger explosion soon after the event and then nine months later:
- Some participants remembered accurately, but others were less accurate and there were discrepancies between initial memories and what was remembered nine months later.
- Suggests that so-called FBs can be subject to the same sort of inaccuracies and forgetting as any other kind of long-term memory.

- Wright (1993) found that people had poor recall for the Hillsborough football stadium disaster. After five months, recall was based on reconstructions, i.e. blending real memories with things they had been told or had read in the press.

EVALUATION OF FLASHBULB MEMORIES – DO THEY REALLY EXIST?

- People do remember things about important events for a long time afterwards but it is difficult to judge whether these memories are accurate.
- Neisser (1978) has suggested that FBs are not encoded differently, as Brown and Kulik thought. He says that they are long-lasting simply because such events are often talked about and revisited in conversation and in the media.
- Some research studies have failed to demonstrate FBs convincingly.
- Conway (1995) defends the concept of FBs – he says that the studies which fail to show it have not used events that meet the criteria for FBs, i.e. ones that have great personal significance.

- Conway et al. (1994) interviewed students about their personal memories around the resignation of Margaret Thatcher – found that British students had much more accurate recall after 11 months than foreign students. Suggests that the event met the criteria in the UK.

REPRESSION

DEFINITION

Repression is a defence mechanism first described by Freud. It is an unconscious process that ensures threatening or anxiety-provoking memories are kept from conscious awareness.

IS THERE ANY EVIDENCE FOR REPRESSION?

Freud developed the idea of repression while treating patients. He reported examples of repression in his case studies, i.e. in accounts/observations of his patients. It is much more difficult to demonstrate an unconscious behaviour in a well controlled laboratory study.

SOME RESEARCH ATTEMPTS TO INVESTIGATE REPRESSION

Laboratory study

Levinger and Clark (1961) asked participants to generate associations to lists of emotionally charged or neutral words. They gave participants cued recall test.

- Found that emotional words took longer to be generated, were less well recalled and produced higher GSRs than neutral words.

- Suggests emotional words cause anxiety (shown by higher GSR) and that they were repressed (shown by poorer recall).

Natural study

Williams (1992) interviewed about 100 women who had been treated in ER for sexual abuse as children.

- Found that 38% had no recall of abuse.

- 16% of remainder said that they had forgotten the abuse at some time in their lives. The younger the child at time of abuse, the more likely the memory was forgotten.

- Suggests that painful memories are repressed, but can sometimes be retrieved.

SOME USEFUL POINTS TO INCLUDE IN AN EVALUATION OF REPRESSION

It is difficult to provide convincing evidence of repression because:

- Repression is used to bury traumatic memories – it is difficult to produce such traumatic events in the laboratory.

- It is not only difficult to produce traumatic events – it would also be **unethical**.

- By definition, it is difficult to retrieve repressed memories (they are repressed because they are too painful to face up to), so how do we know what has been repressed in the first place?

- If so-called repressed memories are recovered, there is some doubt about their reliability.

- Levinger and Clark (1961) did not manage this in their experiment.

- Freud's case studies are based on his speculation about what has been repressed.

- This refers to the idea of false memory syndrome. Loftus (1997), for example, has shown that false memories can be planted on people. For example, she arranged for a 14-year old boy to be told by his older brother that he had been lost in a shopping centre when he was a young child. The younger brother started to remember details of this event within two weeks of having been told about it – even though it had never actually happened!

TYPICAL QUESTIONS...

AO1 QUESTIONS

1 What is meant by the terms 'flashbulb memories' and 'repression'? (3 + 3 marks)

Must make it clear to examiners which term is being explained and need to write enough for 3 marks for each one.

2 Outline research findings into the role of emotional factors in memory. (6 marks)

*Emphasis on findings and not procedures. Could use material on **either** FBs **or** repression **or** both.*

3 Explain what is meant by flashbulb memories and give one criticism of them. (3 + 3 marks)

This kind of question might also refer to repression.

AO1 + AO2 QUESTIONS

4 Outline and evaluate research that investigates emotional factors in memory. (18 marks)

5 Discuss research into flashbulb memories. (18 marks)

CRITICAL ISSUE: EYEWITNESS TESTIMONY (I)

MUST KNOW...
• Reconstructive memory and associated research.

RECONSTRUCTIVE MEMORY

DEFINITION

The term reconstructive memory is usually associated with Bartlett. It is memory which is distorted by the individual's prior knowledge and expectations.

A **schema** is a knowledge package built up through experience of the world which can help us to understand and interpret new information.

WHAT BARTLETT BELIEVED

• Memory is an active process.
• We do not store exact replicas of the initial stimulus.
• We weave in elements of existing knowledge and experience (schemas).
• We form these elements into a coherent whole.
• This means that what we actually remember may not be an accurate reproduction of the original stimulus.

MUST REMEMBER...
One study **in detail** (APFCC) on reconstructive memory, but need to know some findings from other relevant research.

APFCC STUDY: BARTLETT (1932)	
A	To see how cultural expectations affect memory.
P	• Read out an unfamiliar folk story to participants. • After 20 hours, participants asked to retell the story. • Participants were asked several more times to recall the story over an extended period of time. • Bartlett kept a record of successive recall for each participant (protocols).
F	• The recalled story was distorted in several different ways. • Distortions became more pronounced over time.
C	• Story was being changed to fit in with participants' own experience and so became easier to remember. • The memory reconstruction process continues over time, i.e. the memory goes on changing.
C	• Influential study that helped us to understand why memories can be inaccurate. This study was poorly controlled and designed, e.g. participants not given very clear instructions; there were no independent judges of the protocols – Bartlett may have been biased in the way he interpreted the data.

• Called *The War of the Ghosts* – a North American Folk tale full of words and ideas that would be unfamiliar to Bartlett's participants.

• Bartlett recorded:
  – rationalisations
  – omissions
  – changes of order
  – alterations in importance
  – distortions of emotions.

• Gauld and Stephenson (1967) found distortions and errors were significantly reduced when people were specifically instructed to recall the story accurately.

MUST REMEMBER...
That criticisms can be positive as well as negative.

RELATED RESEARCH SHOWING SUPPORT FOR THE EFFECT OF SCHEMAS ON RECALL

- List (1986) asked people to rate various events in terms of probability in a shoplifting scenario. She then showed different participants a shoplifting video and then tested their recall a week later. She found that recall was better for high-probability events than low-probability events and that, where events were falsely recalled, they were more likely to be high-probability.

- Brewer and Treyens (1981) found that people were often inaccurate when unexpectedly asked to name items in an office where they had waited for 35 seconds. They falsely recalled items that could have been expected in an office (high schema expectancy) but were not actually there and tended not to recall items with low schema expectancy.

- Bransford and Johnson (1972) found that people could recall a passage of ambiguous text better if they were given a title or picture beforehand that helped to make the passage more meaningful.

However…
Some highly unexpected items, e.g. a skull, were recalled by some people. Difficult to explain by schema theory.

SUMMARY EVALUATION OF RECONSTRUCTIVE MEMORY

Strengths	Limitations
• Explains why we are sometimes inaccurate at recalling events – particularly important with reference to eyewitness testimony.	• Bartlett's own research, though imaginative, was poorly controlled.
• Large body of research evidence to support the idea that memories can be reconstructed (see above).	• Memory can be very accurate under some circumstances – we clearly do not always reconstruct.
• Research is often based on more real-life situations (e.g. List) than some other memory research that uses letters and digits as stimulus material.	• The idea of schemas is useful, but it is quite a vague concept and we do not know how schemas are acquired in the first place.

For practice in answering AS Psychology questions, why not use *Collins Exam Practice AS Psychology*?

TYPICAL QUESTIONS...

AO1 QUESTIONS

1 What is meant by the term 'reconstructive memory' and give one criticism of this concept? (3 + 3 marks)

Need slightly more detail for a 3-mark definition than a 2-mark definition.

2 Describe the procedures and findings of one study of reconstructive memory. (6 marks)

This kind of question can ask for any two from APFC. Do not have to give equal weight to the two parts of the study.

3 Describe the conclusions of one study of reconstructive memory and give one criticism of this study. (3 + 3 marks)

*This kind of question could ask for any one of APFC.
NB Conclusions and findings are different!*

AO1 + AO2 QUESTIONS

4 Outline and evaluate research into reconstructive memory. (18 marks)

The focus here is on research. Must not waste time on definitions. Focus on findings and conclusions. Must not get bogged down in procedural detail. Remember the AO1/AO2 split. AO1 = 6 marks, AO2 = 12 marks.

5 'We do not passively record memories as if we were taking a photo. Instead, we try to make more sense of events by blending them with our previous experiences and knowledge.' Discuss research that investigates reconstructive memory. (18 marks)

The quotation is there to help – must not waste time writing it out and do not need to refer to it.

CRITICAL ISSUE: EYEWITNESS TESTIMONY (2)

EYEWITNESS TESTIMONY (EWT)

DEFINITION

Eyewitness testimony or EWT is the evidence given in court or in police investigations by someone who has witnessed a crime or an accident.

WHY STUDY EWT?

Defendants are often convicted on the basis of EWT alone and yet it seems that EWT is not always reliable. It is important for psychologists to find out **why** it is inaccurate and **how to improve accuracy.**

DEFINITION

A leading question is a question about an event that is phrased in such a way that it prompts a particular answer. Information is provided in the question (i.e. *after* the event) which may distort the accuracy of the memory.

Examples of leading questions
- 'Did you see the broken glass?' (Use of 'the' implies that there was broken glass.)
- 'How fast was the car going when it smashed into another car?' (Use of the word 'smashed' implies quite high speed.)

MUST REMEMBER...
One study **in detail** (APFCC) on leading questions in EWT, but need to know some findings from other relevant research.

- However, the participants were all students – not a representative sample.

- They might have guessed what was expected, i.e. there might have been **demand characteristics**.

APFCC STUDY: LOFTUS AND PALMER (1974)

A	To investigate the accuracy of memory for a car accident and to see whether leading questions affect accuracy.
P	• Showed films of traffic accidents to 45 participants. • After watching, participants had to answer a series of questions about what they had seen. • Participants were divided into five groups – all filled in same questionnaire apart from one critical question which was different for each group. • The mean speed estimate was calculated for each group.
F	• The mean speed varied significantly between groups. • 'smashed' = approx. 41 m.p.h., 'collided' = approx. 40 m.p.h., 'bumped' = approx. 38 m.p.h., 'hit' = approx. 34 m.p.h., 'contacted' = approx. 32 m.p.h.
C	• The wording of the question can affect the accuracy of the answer.
C	• People were expecting to witness a car accident. In real life, an accident is likely to be unexpected. • Real eyewitnesses are likely to be emotionally affected and will also know that their testimony could have serious consequences.

- **Critical question**
  About how fast were the cars going when they **hit** each other? For each of the other four groups the word 'hit' was replaced by:
  – 'smashed into'
  – 'collided with'
  – 'bumped into'
  – 'contacted'.

- Loftus and Palmer (1974) did a similar study only using the words 'hit', 'smashed' and a control condition (no question about speed). A week later, they asked the question 'Did you see any broken glass?' (There was none.) More people mistakenly recalled broken glass in the 'smashed' condition.

- Foster et al (1994) found that people were much more accurate in their memory of a bank robbery when they were led to believe that their testimony would influence a real trial.

RELATED RESEARCH INTO LEADING QUESTIONS

Loftus (1975):
- Two groups watched the same film of a car accident and then answered 10 questions. The questions were the same for each group apart from one. (Group 1 had a question consistent with the film, Group 2 had a different question which contained misleading information about a barn.)
  – A week later, both groups answered 10 more questions – the final question was 'Did you see a barn?'
  – More people in Group 2 gave the incorrect answer 'Yes'.

IS EWT ALWAYS INACCURATE?

Loftus has made a huge contribution to our understanding of EWT and her research is very rigorous. It is clear that memory can sometimes be altered in the light of misleading post-event information or because of factors such as anxiety. However, is EWT always as inaccurate as her studies show?

- Loftus found that people are less accurate at identifying faces in emotionally arousing circumstances than in non-threatening circumstances (weapons effect).

HOWEVER...
Christianson and Hubinette (1993) found that witnesses of real life crimes were actually more accurate than people who had been less directly threatened.

- Loftus found that people can be misled by the types of questions they are asked.

HOWEVER...
It is important to note that **not everyone** is misled (e.g. in the 'barn' experiment, only 17% of the misled group believed later that they had really seen a non-existent barn).

- Loftus found that post-event information can distort the original memory.

HOWEVER...
Loftus herself showed that there are limits to what can be suggested. If the information is blatantly wrong (e.g. a red purse described as brown), people are not fooled and do not alter their original memory.

- Loftus found that people are often misled into picking the wrong answer on questionnaires testing their recall for events.

HOWEVER...
She often used forced-choice formats on her questionnaires. Koriat and Goldsmith (1996) found that witness accuracy increases hugely if recall tests do not rely on a forced choice and if questions are asked in a more logical order.

TYPICAL QUESTIONS...

AO1 QUESTIONS

1 What is meant by the terms 'eyewitness testimony' and 'leading questions'? (3 + 3 marks)

This could also be a 2 + 2 + 2 question and include 'reconstructive memory' as a third definition.

2 Describe the procedures and conclusions of one study of leading questions. (6 marks)

This kind of question can ask for any two from APFC.

3 Describe the findings of one study of eyewitness testimony and give one criticism of the study. (3 + 3 marks)

This kind of question can ask for any two from APFC plus one criticism. Criticisms can be positive as well as negative.

AO1 + AO2 QUESTIONS

4 Outline and evaluate research into eyewitness testimony. (18 marks)

Where the question asks for EWT research, this is not restricted to leading questions studies.

5 'Juries should not rely on eyewitness testimony because it is so inaccurate.' To what extent does research show that eyewitness testimony is inaccurate? (18 marks)

MUST REMEMBER...
That material on reconstructive memory can be used to explain why memories for events might be inaccurate (i.e. because of schemas) but that studies by Bartlett are **not** EWT studies.

STAGES IN THE FORMATION OF ATTACHMENTS

DEFINITION
Attachments are strong emotional bonds between an infant and its caregiver.

→

Must be able to expand this definition for a 3-mark question.

→

EXPANSION
- Attachments maintain proximity between infant and caregiver and are important for subsequent emotional development.

PHASES IN THE DEVELOPMENT OF ATTACHMENT (BOWLBY, 1969)
- Pre-attachments (0–2 months): indiscriminate social responsiveness – infants produce the same responses to all objects, animate or inanimate.
- Attachment in the making (2–6 months): recognition of familiar people – infants prefer human company and can distinguish between familiar and unfamiliar people. Don't yet show anxiety with strangers.
- Specific attachments (around 6 months): separation protest and stranger anxiety – infants show attachment to one particular person and protest when separated from them. They also begin to display stranger anxiety.
- Goal-corrected partnership (2 years onwards): relationships become two-sided – infant learns to predict the mother's behaviour, and each of them adjusts their behaviour to the needs of the other.

Exact ages aren't necessary but sequence and approximate ages are.

WHAT INFLUENCES ATTACHMENT (SCHAFFER AND EMERSON, 1964)
- Age at first attachment: They found that most children form their first attachment between 6 and 8 months and show separation anxiety when separated from this person. Fear of strangers develops about one month after this.
- Attachment figures: After the main attachment is formed, children then form attachments to others, with very few being attached to just one person at 18 months.
  In most children the mother is the primary attachment figure, with fathers rarely being
  the sole attachment figure.
- Strength of attachment: This peaks in the first month after the attachment bond develops but there are large individual differences. Intensely attached children had mothers who responded quickly to their demands and offered the most interaction.
- Time spent with infant: The person who spent most time with the child (i.e. fed, bathed and changed them) was not necessarily the one with whom they developed their primary attachment. This tended to be with the mother even though it might not be her performing these tasks.

CONCLUSION
1 Attachment to a specific person forms around 7 months.
2 Multiple attachments develop soon afterwards.
3 Attachments seem to form with those who are responsive to the child rather than just spend time with them.

EVALUATION OF BOWLBY'S PHASE ACCOUNT

1 Some aspects of Bowlby's model **may not be accurate**, with very young infants being more social than originally thought, recognising their caregivers at an earlier age.

▶ • e.g. Bushell et al. (1989) found that infants less than 24 hours looked longer at their mother than another woman.

2 Close agreement regarding the appearance of **separation anxiety** (research evidence by Schaffer, 1998).

▶ • This might be explained in terms of children's cognitive development, particularly the emergence of object permanence.

3 Attachment can also be explained in terms of **physical development**, i.e. attachment develops at a time when children first become mobile.

▶ • Ainsworth (1967) found that Ugandan babies attach earlier but also become mobile earlier.

This is important because it shows that attachment and motor development are linked.

▼

So **there is support** for the claim that some sort of attachment appears around the age of 6 months, although the process of attachment may begin at birth.

MUST TAKE CARE...
To elaborate critical points as this brings higher marks.

For practice in answering AS Psychology questions, why not use *Collins Exam Practice AS Psychology*?

TYPICAL QUESTIONS...

AO1 QUESTIONS

1 What is meant by the term 'attachment' in the context of child development? (2 marks)

2 Explain what is meant by the term 'attachment' in the context of developmental psychology. (3 marks)   *This requires the 2-mark version plus the expansion material.*

3 Outline stages in the formation of attachments. (6 marks)   *Don't need to worry too much about the ages or even the 'label' for each stage.*

4 Outline two factors that influence the formation of attachments. (3 + 3 marks)

5 Outline findings of research into the formation of attachments. (6 marks)

6 Outline the formation of attachments. (6 marks)   *This is a wide open question, so could focus on stages, research, factors that influence attachment, etc.*

AO1 + AO2 QUESTION

7 Outline and evaluate research into the formation of attachments. (18 marks)

SECURE AND INSECURE ATTACHMENTS

DEFINITION

Secure attachment: the optimal form of attachment, associated with healthy emotional and social development.

Insecure attachment: a less optimal form of attachment – insecurely attached infants show disturbed behaviour during separation and reunion.

Must be able to expand these definitions for 3-mark questions.

EXPANSION

- Securely attached infants feel content to explore a strange environment using their caregiver as a safe base.
- Insecurely attached children tend to have less successful relationships with peers and others later in life.

DIFFERENCES BETWEEN SECURE AND INSECURE ATTACHMENT

- Secure attachment develops as a result of **caregivers' constant and sensitive responding** to the infant's needs, whereas insecure attachment develops when this is absent.
- Securely attached infants seek out and are comfortable with **social interaction and intimacy** whereas insecurely attached infants tend to avoid social interaction or both seek and reject others.

RESEARCH STUDY (AINSWORTH AND BELL, 1970)

Aims
- Aimed to assess quality of attachment by placing an infant in a situation of mild stress (to encourage the infant to seek comfort) and novelty (to encourage exploration).
- Both are indicators of the quality of attachment.

Procedures
- 100 middle-class American infants and their mothers took part.
- Infants and their mothers observed in the eight sessions of the 'Strange Situation', with each session lasting three minutes.
- Observers recorded infants' and mothers' behaviours noting: separation anxiety, infant's willingness to explore, stranger anxiety and reunion behaviour.

Findings
Infants were classified into three broad groups:
- Type B (securely attached – about 66%). They explored the unfamiliar room, were subdued when their mother left and greeted her positively when she returned. Showed moderate avoidance of the stranger. Mothers were described as sensitive.
- Type A (avoidant-insecure – about 22%). Did not approach their mother during exploration, seemed unconcerned by her absence and showed little interest when she returned. They avoided the stranger but avoided mother more on return. These mothers tended to ignore their infants.
- Type C (resistant-insecure – about 12%). Showed intense distress, particularly when mother was absent, but rejected her on her return. Showed ambivalent behaviour towards the stranger. These mothers appeared to behave ambivalently towards their infants.

Conclusions
- Study demonstrates significant individual differences between infants.
- Shows that most American children are securely attached.
- Shows an association between mothers' behaviour and infants' attachment type, suggesting that mothers' behaviour is important in determining attachment type.

CRITICISM

It would be unreasonable to make generalisations about *all* infant behaviour on the basis of just this sample (middle-class American infants and their mothers). This can only tell us about how *this* group behaves, i.e. it lacks **population validity**.

It's rare to get asked for more than one criticism, so just one should be okay. However – must be able to elaborate on this!

OTHER RESEARCH ON SECURE AND INSECURE ATTACHMENT

- Wartner et al. (1994) found that using the Strange Situation classification (SSC), children tended to be classified in the same way at different ages (this showed that the classification was reliable).

- Lamb (1977) found children behave differently depending on who they are with – they may have a secure attachment with one parent and an avoidant one with the other (suggesting that the SSC measures particular attachments rather than general attachment style).

- Isabella et al. (1989) found mothers and infants who were responsive to each other at 1 month were more likely to have a secure relationship at 12 months. A one-sided pattern of interaction was more likely to result in an insecure relationship (supports the caregiver sensitivity hypothesis, that attachment depends on warm and loving responsiveness of the caregiver).

MUST REMEMBER...
To make sure that answers are sufficiently detailed (to get higher marks) – therefore must not include too many studies in response to a question on 'research' in this area.

The conclusions from these studies turn this material into AO2 commentary.

Questions could ask for conclusions of research into secure and insecure attachment instead of findings. Need to practise turning findings into conclusions (difference = the difference between what was found and the conclusions that can be drawn from that finding).

Conclusions can be multi-purpose. They can be AO1 in APFCC questions and 'conclusions' of research questions, but AO2 in AO1 + AO2 questions!

THE STRANGE SITUATION

What happens in the Strange Situation:

1 Mother and child are introduced to the room.

2 Mother and child are left alone and the child can investigate the toys.

3 A stranger enters the room and talks with the mother. The stranger gradually approaches the infant with a toy.

4 Mother leaves the child alone with the stranger, and the stranger interacts with the child.

5 Mother returns to greet and comfort the child.

6 The child is left on its own.

7 The stranger returns and tries to engage with the child.

8 Mother returns, greets and picks up the child. The stranger leaves inconspicuously.

TYPICAL QUESTIONS...

AO1 QUESTIONS

1 Explain what is meant by 'secure attachment' and 'insecure attachment'. (3 + 3 marks)

2 What is meant by the terms 'secure attachment' and 'insecure attachment', and give one difference between them? (2 + 2 + 2 marks)

3 Describe the aims and findings of one study of individual differences in attachment. (6 marks)

4 Describe the aims and procedures of one study of individual differences in attachment. (6 marks)

5 Describe the findings of one study of individual differences in attachment and give one criticism of this study. (6 marks)

6 Outline findings of research into cross-cultural variations in attachment. (6 marks)

These are APFCC questions (i.e. aims, procedures, findings, etc.). Need to write about 100 or so words for these questions, but could be 25 words for the aims and 75 for the procedures, etc.

AO1 + AO2 QUESTION

7 Outline and evaluate research into secure and insecure attachment. (18 marks)

CROSS-CULTURAL VARIATIONS IN ATTACHMENT

DEFINITION

Cross-cultural variations are differences in beliefs and practices, particularly related to child-rearing between people of different cultures.

EXPANSION
• These beliefs and practices may influence the kinds of attachments that people from different cultures have with their children.

What's a culture?

Not just a group of people, but all the beliefs and customs that people in a particular society share.

Specification only requires a study on individual differences, so could use this study or the study of secure and insecure attachment.

RESEARCH STUDY OF CROSS-CULTURAL VARIATIONS IN ATTACHMENT (TAKAHASHI, 1990)

Aim

To see whether the Strange Situation is a valid procedure for assessing attachment style in cultures other than the US, in this case Japanese mothers and their children.

Procedures
• Participants were 60 middle-class Japanese infants (aged 1 year) and their mothers.
• Infants and mothers were observed in the Strange Situation to assess their willingness to explore, their reaction to their mother leaving and returning and their reaction to a stranger.

Findings
• Two-thirds of the children were securely attached (same as the American sample).
• No infants were avoidant-insecure.
• One-third of the infants were resistant-insecure.
• Some differences with American sample – Japanese infants more disturbed when left alone.

Conclusions
• Findings suggest there are cross-cultural differences in the way infants respond to separation.
• Total lack of avoidant behaviour in Japanese sample which might be explained in terms of socialisation differences between Japanese and American cultures.
• Strange Situation does not have the same meaning for Japanese infants who responded as if extremely stressed.

CRITICISM 1

This study was carried out on a limited sample of only middle-class, home-reared infants, and so it may not be possible to generalise findings to all Japanese children (i.e. lacks **population validity**).

CRITICISM 2

Research with very young children has the potential for causing significant psychological harm to participants; therefore there are important **ethical considerations** with research of this nature.

EXPANSION

Although Takahashi stopped observations when infants became too distressed, the study itself was not stopped even though it became obvious that extreme distress was likely.

These can be used in conjunction with the Takahashi study for questions on research findings and/or conclusions.

OTHER RESEARCH FINDINGS ON CROSS-CULTURAL VARIATIONS

- Van IJzendoorn and Kroonenberg (1988) found evidence of considerable consistency across cultures in terms of attachment styles.

  They found that the similarity between countries may be due to the increasing effects of the mass media rather than other cultural differences.

- Grossmann and Grossmann (1991) found that German infants were more likely to be classified as insecurely attached rather than securely attached.

OTHER CONCLUSIONS FROM RESEARCH ON CROSS-CULTURAL RESEARCH

- Van IJzendoorn and Kroonenberg conclude that the same caregiver–infant interactions contribute to secure and insecure attachments in all cultures.
- The Grossmann and Grossmann findings may be related to the German cultural norm of keeping some interpersonal distance between parents and children. As a result, infants don't engage in proximity-seeking behaviour and so *appear* to be insecurely attached.

MUST TAKE CARE...

If a question asks for research **findings** then don't include anything about procedures.

Useful for questions on research findings, but no need to include all this information.

Criticisms count as AO1 in part (a) and part (b) questions, but as AO2 in part (c) questions.

CROSS-CULTURAL DIFFERENCES IN SECURE AND INSECURE ATTACHMENT

Country	No. of studies	Percentage of each attachment type (to the nearest whole number)		
		Secure	Avoidant	Resistant
West Germany	3	57	35	8
Great Britain	1	75	22	3
Netherlands	4	67	26	7
Sweden	1	74	22	4
Israel	2	64	7	29
Japan	2	68	5	27
China	1	50	25	25
United States	18	65	21	14
Overall average		65	21	14

Source: Van IJzendoorn and Kroonenberg (1988, pages 150–51)

Questions *could* ask for **criticisms** of research into cross-cultural variations:

- Strange Situation assumes that **independence** is a sign of secure attachment, but this may not apply to collectivist societies where **interdependence** is more important. So the SS may not be a valid measure in these societies.
- Some studies have only used middle-class infants so it is difficult to generalise out to all members of a culture, or to make valid conclusions about cross-cultural variations.

TYPICAL QUESTIONS...

AO1 QUESTIONS

1 What is meant by 'cross-cultural variations' in attachment? (2 marks)

2 Explain what is meant by 'cross-cultural variations' in attachment. (3 marks)

Examiners have to discriminate between 1, 2 and 3 mark answers, so by saying three things it makes it easier for them to award all 3 marks!

3 Describe the aims and procedures of one study of individual differences in attachment. (6 marks)

4 Describe the findings and conclusions of one study of individual differences in attachment. (6 marks)

5 Describe the findings of one study of individual differences in attachment and give one criticism of this study. (6 marks)

6 Outline findings of research into cross-cultural variations in attachment. (6 marks)

AO1 + AO2 QUESTION

7 To what extent has research shown that there are cross-cultural variations in attachment? (18 marks)

EXPLANATIONS OF ATTACHMENT

EXPLANATION I – LEARNING THEORY

OUTLINE OF EXPLANATION

1 Attachment is learned through classical conditioning – mother becomes associated with food (which is pleasant).

2 Attachment is learned through operant conditioning – mother becomes a source of reward (i.e. a secondary reinforcer).

3 Infant therefore becomes attached to the person who feeds them.

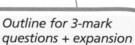

EXPANSION

• The food-giver becomes a source of pleasure by association *regardless* of whether food is being given.

• Because the mother is a source of reward, the infant seeks to be with her.

• This is also known as the 'cupboard-love' theory because it suggests attachment is based solely on the satisfaction of this basic need.

Outline for 3-mark questions + expansion for 6-mark questions.

EVALUATION

• Schaffer and Emerson (1964) found that less than half of infants had a primary attachment to the person who usually fed them.

▷ • This challenges the learning theory prediction of attachment being linked to feeding.

• Harlow and Harlow (1962) found that contact comfort was more important for attachment.

▷ • We should be cautious about making generalisations about human behaviour from studies of animals.

MUST REMEMBER...
That higher marks are awarded when critical points are **elaborated**, so should first identify a critical point and then elaborate it.

• Learning theories are criticised for being reductionist, reducing complex human behaviour to simple relationships.

▷ • Therefore it is possible that these explanations are too simple to explain a complex behaviour like attachment.

EXPLANATION 2 – BOWLBY'S THEORY

OUTLINE OF EXPLANATION

1 Infants are innately programmed to form an attachment and adults are innately programmed to respond to their infants.

2 As attachment is a biological process, it takes place during a critical period of development, or not at all.

3 Attachment plays a role in later development because it provides a template for relationships.

Outline for 3-mark questions + expansion for 6-mark questions

EXPANSION

- Bowlby suggested that social behaviours such as smiling and crying are innate in infants and the resulting caring response is innate in adults.
- Bowlby suggested that if a child does not form an attachment before the age of 2½ years, it would not be possible after this age.
- The child's relationship with their primary attachment figure provides them with an internal working model of themselves which influences their later relationships.

MUST TAKE CARE...
Not to confuse Bowlby's theory of attachment with his theory of deprivation.

EVALUATION

- Sroufe et al (1999) found that children rated as securely attached in infancy showed high levels of social competence in adolescence.

- This supports Bowlby's views of continuity from infancy to adulthood in terms of social development.

MUST REMEMBER...
Critical points can be *positive* as well as negative.

- This continuity in development can be explained without using Bowlby's ideas about attachment.

- Possible that some children are born more trusting and friendly, which is why they become securely attached and form relationships more easily (temperament hypothesis).

These studies are 'borrowed' from a later section to reinforce the point being made. This is allowed.

- Theory cannot explain why some children are able to cope with poor attachment experiences while others suffer long-term consequences.

- Study of Czech twins showed that despite lack of attachment they developed normally, but Curtiss (1977) found that the girl Genie never achieved good social adjustment after early privation.

TYPICAL QUESTIONS...

AO1 QUESTIONS

1 Outline **two** explanations of attachment. (3 + 3 marks)

Learning theory would be one explanation and Bowlby's theory the other.

2 Describe **one** explanation of attachment. (6 marks)

3 Outline **one** explanation of attachment and give one criticism of this explanation. (3 + 3 marks)

4 Give **two** criticisms of one explanation of attachment. (3+ 3 marks)

AO1 + AO2 QUESTION
Outline and evaluate **one or more** explanation of attachment. (18 marks)

*Could just use **one** explanation here instead of two, but would then need about 200 words of evaluation for that explanation, so easier to use two.*

BOWLBY'S MATERNAL DEPRIVATION HYPOTHESIS

MUST KNOW...
- Bowlby's deprivation hypothesis and criticisms of this.
- Research evidence on which this hypothesis is based.

DEFINITION

Deprivation refers to the loss of emotional care, which results in the breaking of emotional bonds.

EXPANSION
- Bowlby believed that this disrupts the attachment process, which may harm emotional and social development.

MUST REMEMBER...

Bowlby's maternal hypothesis states that: 'If an infant was unable to form a warm, intimate and continuous relationship with the mother (or substitute), then they would have difficulty forming relationships with others and be more at risk of behavioural disorders.'

WHAT DOES IT INVOLVE?

MUST TAKE CARE...

Not to confuse **this** hypothesis with Bowlby's theory of attachment!

THE MATERNAL DEPRIVATION HYPOTHESIS (Bowlby, 1953)

A continuous relationship with the mother is vital.

The development of this continuous relationship must occur within a critical period.

Child needs a relationship with one primary caregiver (monotropy).

Discontinuous relationships become unstable and disrupt the development.

Repeated separations before age of 2½ most damaging although child still vulnerable up to age 5.

This is most likely to be the child's mother, but does not have to be.

CRITICISMS OF BOWLBY'S MATERNAL DEPRIVATION HYPOTHESIS

Positive criticisms

1 Bowlby's hypothesis identified the importance of emotional care in the healthy emotional care of the child. Prior to that time it had been believed that a good standard of physical care was all that was needed.

2 This changed the treatment of children in hospitals. Parents are now encouraged to stay overnight with their children, because this prevents emotional deprivation and promotes faster recovery through a reduction of anxiety.

Negative criticisms

1 Bowlby confused cause and effect. Rutter (1981) claimed that the fact that early deprivation and later maladjustment are linked is because some families are at risk of both due to poor living conditions or unsettled personal relationships.

2 Bowlby did not distinguish between the effects of deprivation, where attachment bonds are formed but broken, and privation, where no bond is ever formed. Rutter claimed that it is privation that is more damaging for future development.

Criticisms can be either positive or negative, so any of these can be used as evaluation of Bowlby's hypothesis.

EVIDENCE ON WHICH BOWLBY'S VIEWS ARE BASED

Bowlby (1944) wanted to see if frequent early separations were associated with the development of affectionless psychopathy.

- He found that a large number of juvenile thieves diagnosed as affectionless psychopaths had experienced early and prolonged separations from their mothers.
- The percentage of thieves without affectionless psychopathy who had experienced similar early separations was much lower.

Spitz and Wolf (1946) studied 100 children who became depressed after staying in hospital.

- They found that the children generally recovered well if the separation was less than three months.
- The recovery rate for those who had experienced longer separations was much lower.

POSITIVE EVALUATION

- Bowlby's conclusion that these findings suggest a link between early separations and later maladjustment are supported by research by Skeels and Dye (1939). They found that orphans who received replacement emotional care from mentally retarded women showed reduced maladjustment later in life.

NEGATIVE EVALUATION

- Bowlby's evidence is only correlational, which means that although early separation and affectionless psychopathy are linked in some way, we cannot say one caused the other.
- The data on separation was collected retrospectively so may not be reliable. We don't know if these children had suitable emotional care during their separation.

ROBERTSON AND ROBERTSON (1971)

The Robertsons filmed children under the age of 3 during short separations:
- John – spent nine days in a residential nursery. The staff did not attend to his emotional needs, and he was overwhelmed by the strange environment. He showed maladjustment for months after the experience. This supports Bowlby's research because separations during a sensitive phase of development were followed by later maladjustment.

MUST REMEMBER...

To make sure that answers are sufficiently detailed (to get higher marks) – therefore must not include too many studies in response to a question on 'research' in this area.

However...

Several other children were cared for by a foster mother during their separation from their primary care-giver. These children showed none of the ill effects seen in John. **This suggests that if the child's emotional needs are met during separation, then they tend not to suffer in the long-term.**

For practice in answering AS Psychology questions, why not use *Collins Exam Practice AS Psychology*?

TYPICAL QUESTIONS...

AOL QUESTIONS

1 What is meant by 'maternal deprivation'? (2 marks)

2 Explain what is meant by 'maternal deprivation'. (3 marks)

3 Outline Bowlby's maternal deprivation hypothesis. (6 marks)

4 Outline evidence on which Bowlby's maternal deprivation hypothesis is based. (6 marks)

5 Give two criticisms of Bowlby's maternal deprivation hypothesis. (3 + 3 marks)

6 Give two criticisms of evidence on which Bowlby's maternal deprivation hypothesis is based. (3 + 3 marks)

AO1 + AO2 QUESTIONS

7 Outline and evaluate Bowlby's maternal deprivation hypothesis. (18 marks)

8 Outline and evaluate evidence on which Bowlby's maternal deprivation hypothesis is based. (18 marks)

THE EFFECTS OF PRIVATION

DEFINITION
Privation refers to a complete lack of emotional care, leading to no attachments being formed.

→

EXPANSION
• This lack of early attachment is thought to result in permanent harm to emotional and social development.

Privation and deprivation differ – privation means that no attachment bond has been formed whereas deprivation means that the bond has formed but has been broken.

RESEARCH EVIDENCE ON THE EFFECTS OF PRIVATION

Longitudinal studies of children in institutional care	Case histories of children in extreme isolation	Studies of reactive attachment disorder
e.g. Hodges and Tizard (1989)	e.g. Genie (Curtiss, 1977), Czech twins (Koluchová, 1976)	e.g. Parker and Forrest (1993)

Found that the cause of this disorder is a lack of primary attachments due to maternal rejection and separation.

Aims
To investigate the effects of early privation of subsequent social and emotional development by following the same children over a long period of time.

Procedures
• Participants were 65 children put in an institution when less than 4 months old.
• At age 4, 24 of the children had been adopted, 15 returned to their natural homes (the 'restored' group), and the rest remained in the institution.
• Adopted and restored children were assessed at age 8 and again at age 16, with data also obtained from a control group.

Findings
• **Some differences:** adopted children had close attachments to parents and good family relationships (not true for the 'restored' children).
• **Some similarities:** both adopted and restored children more likely to seek adult attention and approval than controls. Both groups less successful in peer relationships.

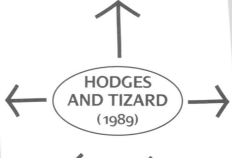

HODGES AND TIZARD (1989)

Conclusions
• Findings suggest that the children showed **permanent damage** as a result of their early institutional life, particularly in terms of their ability to form relationships outside the family.
• Fact that the restored group had close attachments after returning to their family shows that **recovery from privation is possible**.

Criticism
• Possible that children selected for adopted and restored groups differed in ways that influenced their reaction to privation. Because these **individual differences** were uncontrolled, we cannot infer a causal relationship between privation and later development.

CASE HISTORIES OF CHILDREN IN EXTREME ISOLATION

Genie (Curtiss, 1977)
- Found when she was 13 years old.
- Had experienced isolation, severe neglect and physical restraint.
- On discovery made virtually no sounds and was hardly able to walk.
- Never achieved good social adjustment or language despite intervention and being placed with a foster family.

Czech twins (Koluchová, 1976)
- Mother died after birth and put in children's home for 11 months.
- Later went to live with their father (very low IQ) and stepmother (extremely cruel).
- Twins never allowed out and kept in harsh conditions.
- When discovered at age 7, they could hardly walk, were very fearful and speech very poor.
- After being put in foster home made excellent gains and as adults appear well adjusted and cognitively able.

CRITICISM 1

Genie had **abnormal brain wave patterns** – could be a product of the privation but may also have been present at birth, leaving her with learning difficulties which prevented normal development.

CONCLUSION

Some children never recover from early privation but others show remarkable recovery.

MUST TAKE CARE...
Not to include too much detail of privation circumstances if answering a question on **research** findings.

CRITICISM 2

Impossible to generalise from these 'special' case studies. They may have had unique characteristics, making them less useful for understanding how most people would react to privation.

CAN THE EFFECTS OF PRIVATION BE REVERSED?

Quinton et al. (1985)
- Researchers followed a group of women who had grown up in institutions.
- When they became mothers (compared to a group of non-institutionalised mothers), they were less sensitive or supportive to their children, who were more frequently taken into care.
- Although this suggests that the effects of privation are irreversible, maybe that the women had inadequate models for how to parent made them inadequate mothers later on.
- Supported by the finding that those institutionalised mothers who had positive school experiences in childhood and favourable psychosocial circumstances in adulthood functioned as well as the non-institutionalised mothers.

Rutter (1998)
- Studied Romanian orphans adopted in UK before the age of 2.
- Prior to adoption children were physically undersized but had caught up with age-peers by age 4.
- The later the children were adopted, the slower their progress.
- This research shows that the longer children suffer emotional deprivation, the longer it takes them to recover but that recovery is possible.

Curtiss (1977) and Koluchová (1976)
- Some children never recover from early privation but others show remarkable recovery.

- -

TYPICAL QUESTIONS...

AO1 QUESTIONS

1 What is meant by 'privation'? (2 marks)

2 Explain what is meant by 'privation'. (3 marks)

3 Outline two effects of privation. (3 + 3 marks)

4 Outline research into the effects of privation. (6 marks)

5 Outline conclusions of research that has studied whether the effects of privation can be reversed. (6 marks)

6 Give two criticisms of research into the effects of privation. (3 + 3 marks)

AO1 + AO2 QUESTIONS

7 Outline and evaluate research into the effects of privation. (18 marks)

8 To what extent can the effects of privation be reversed? (18 marks)

Must stress two separate **effects**. *These would be:*

1 **Poor adult relationships** *(see Hodges and Tizard study).*

2 **Poor parenting skills** *(see Quinton et al. study).*

THE EFFECTS OF DAY CARE ON CHILDREN'S COGNITIVE DEVELOPMENT

MUST KNOW...
- How day care affects children's cognitive development.

DEFINITIONS

- **Day care** is a form of care for infants and children offered by someone other than close family and taking place outside the home.
- **Cognitive development** refers to the changes that take place with respect to mental abilities such as memory, language and intelligence.

EXPANSION

- Day care differs from institutional care, which refers to long-term 24-hour a day care.
- **Attachment promotes** cognitive development because it offers a secure base for exploration and increased opportunities for stimulation.

TWO EFFECTS OF DAY CARE ON COGNITIVE DEVELOPMENT

Poor-quality care and a lack of stimulation
- If children are not regularly stimulated they find it **difficult to develop a secure and positive sense of self** – necessary for confidence and curiosity.
- Poor-quality care **undermines intellectual and language development** because it fails to provide children with the stimulation they need to learn about the world and how to communicate with others.

The positive effect of high-quality care
- Children who experience high-quality day care benefit in terms of their **cognitive and language development** compared to those who experience poorer-quality care.
- **High-quality care** is characterised by attentive, responsive, affectionate and stimulating caregivers.

MUST TAKE CARE...
Not to confuse **cognitive** with **social** development.

 RESEARCH EVIDENCE: DOES DAY CARE HAVE POSITIVE OR NEGATIVE EFFECTS ON COGNITIVE DEVELOPMENT?

POSITIVE EFFECTS

- Andersson (1992) – children entering day care at an early age performed significantly better on cognitive tests compared to children entering day care at later ages and those in home care.
- Burchinal et al. (1996) – cognitive and language development, and communication skills were found to be positively correlated with the quality of day care.

NEGATIVE EFFECTS

- Bryant et al. (1980) – found that childminders tended to support quiet behaviour, so encouraging passivity and under-stimulation.
- Ruhm (2000) – preschool children had lower reading and maths skills if they had spent time before the age of 3 in day care. After 3 isn't as disruptive although children remain deficient compared to children raised by their own mothers full time until school age.

However...
Harvey (1999) claims that problems detected in children of working mothers at age 3 and 4 may have gone away by age 12.

EVALUATION

Why are the research findings so inconsistent?

There are many factors that influence a child's cognitive development, such as different attachment experiences, quality of day care, gender and different temperaments, so one factor (day care) may not have consistent effects.

Findings are the results of a study but *conclusions* are what the findings mean.

CONCLUSIONS FROM RESEARCH ON DAY CARE AND COGNITIVE DEVELOPMENT

Andersson (1989)

Early day care does not lead to developmental difficulties provided the day care provision is high quality (as it is in Sweden).

Burchinal et al. (1996)

Even small differences in day care quality are related to improved outcomes, particularly for children from impoverished backgrounds.

Bryant et al. (1980)

Some childminders fail to provide a stimulating environment and so the children in their care fail to flourish.

Ruhm (2000)

Children's educational achievement can be significantly held back if their mothers work away from home.

MUST REMEMBER...
That these conclusions can also be used as AO2 but need to embed them as part of a critical commentary.

EVALUATION OF RESEARCH INTO THE EFFECTS OF DAY CARE ON COGNITIVE DEVELOPMENT

Doesn't show a causal relationship

Many of the studies that have shown a relationship between day care and cognitive development **have been correlational only.** This does not show a causal relationship as there may be other contributory factors at work (e.g. family stress, income, temperament of the child).

The importance of the day care environment

Research suggests that there is great **variability in the day care environment** and in caregiver qualities. As a result, the outcomes for each child depend less on the form of care and more on the characteristics of the setting, including staff–child ratios, group size and caregiver stability.

For practice in answering AS Psychology questions, why not use *Collins Exam Practice AS Psychology*?

TYPICAL QUESTIONS...

AOL QUESTIONS

1 What is meant by 'day care'? (2 marks)

2 Explain what is meant by 'day care'. (3 marks)

3 Outline two effects of day care on cognitive development. (3 + 3 marks)

4 Outline research into the effects of day care on cognitive development. (6 marks)

5 Outline findings into the effects of day care on cognitive development. (6 marks)

6 Outline conclusions into the effects of day care on cognitive development. (6 marks)

7 Give two criticisms of research into the effects of day care on cognitive development. (3 + 3 marks)

AO1 + AO2 QUESTIONS

8 Outline and evaluate research into the effects of day care on cognitive development. (18 marks)

9 To what extent has research supported the claim that day care has a negative effect on cognitive development? (18 marks)

THE EFFECTS OF DAY CARE ON CHILDREN'S SOCIAL DEVELOPMENT

MUST KNOW...
• How day care affects social development.

DEFINITION

Social development refers to the changes that take place throughout one's life with respect to social behaviour, such as relationships with friends and family, friendliness and aggressiveness.

EXPANSION

• Attachment promotes social development because it offers an internal working model for conducting relationships with others.

MUST TAKE CARE...
Not to confuse cognitive with social development.

TWO EFFECTS OF DAY CARE ON SOCIAL DEVELOPMENT

The negative effect of poor-quality care
• Some studies indicate that children who have begun day care before their first birthday appear **more assertive, less responsive to adults** and are more avoidant in reunions with parents.
• The longer a child spends in poor-quality day care, the more stress they appear to experience, and this could lead children to become aggressive and disobedient.

The positive effect of high-quality care
• Research suggests that children who attend high-quality day care are **more sociable and popular** when they attend school (Field, 1991). Amount of time spent in day care was positively correlated to the number of friends and extracurricular activities of the children.
• Time spent in day care was positively related to parental ratings of children's leadership, popularity, attractiveness and assertiveness.

Belsky (2003) claims that there is some evidence to suggest that boys and highly negative infants may be more vulnerable to poor-quality day care.

Questions don't ask for positive effects or negative effects, so either or both can be used in an answer.

RESEARCH EVIDENCE: DOES DAY CARE HAVE POSITIVE OR NEGATIVE EFFECTS ON SOCIAL DEVELOPMENT?

POSITIVE EFFECTS

• Clarke-Stewart et al. (1994) – found that children who had attended day care coped better in social situations in their first year at school.
• Schweinhart et al. (1993) – found that children who took part in the Perry Preschool Project had lower delinquency rates and less likelihood of an adult criminal record compared to a control group who didn't take part in the project.

NEGATIVE EFFECTS

• Belsky and Rovine (1988) – Children who spend more than 20 hours per week in day care more insecurely-attached than home-cared children.
• NICHD study (2001) – Children who had spent more than 10 hours per week in day care were more aggressive in school and at home.

However...
The NICHD study (1997) found that infants with extensive day care did not differ from infants without day care in terms of the amount of distress shown during separations from their mothers in the Strange Situation.

CONCLUSIONS FROM RESEARCH ON DAY CARE AND SOCIAL DEVELOPMENT

Clarke-Stewart et al. (1994)

This study found no evidence of attachment differences between children cared for at home or in day care.

Schweinhart et al. (1993)

These researchers concluded that high-quality day care programmes for young children produce significant long-term benefits.

Belsky and Rovine (1988)

They concluded that full-time infant child care prior to the first birthday puts children at risk for later development.

NICHD study (2001)

The findings of this study suggest that the day care experience had no negative effects on attachment.

Showing how research has helped day care is a positive critical point.

MUST REMEMBER...
That conclusions tend to be more general than findings.

EVALUATIONS OF RESEARCH INTO THE EFFECTS OF DAY CARE ON SOCIAL DEVELOPMENT

Using research to improve day care
Research on day care has been instrumental in the **design of high-quality day care programmes**. In one study (Howes et al., 1998), caregivers were involved in in-service training to increase their sensitivity. Six months after training, the children in their day care programme were more secure and the caregivers rated more sensitive than children and caregivers in a control group.

The limitations of quantitative data
Zimiles (1993) argues that researchers tend to give too much weight to **quantitative information** when judging the results of day care programmes. This can cause people to believe that a conclusion is more certain than it really is. Similarly, much of the work in this area is entirely **correlational**, making it difficult to claim that day care is a cause of either positive or negative effects in development.

Questions sometimes don't ask for cognitive or social development specifically, so could use either.

TYPICAL QUESTIONS...

AO1 QUESTIONS

1 What is meant by 'day care', 'cognitive development' and 'social development'? (2 + 2 + 2 marks)

2 Outline two effects of day care on social development. (3 + 3 marks)

3 Outline research into the effects of day care on social development. (6 marks)

4 Outline findings into the effects of day care on social development. (6 marks)

5 Outline conclusions into the effects of day care on social development. (6 marks)

6 Give two criticisms of research into the effects of day care on social development. (3 + 3 marks)

AO1 + AO2 QUESTIONS

7 Outline and evaluate research into the effects of day care on social development. (18 marks)

8 To what extent has research supported the claim that day care has a positive effect on social development? (18 marks)

THE BODY'S RESPONSE TO STRESSORS

DEFINITION

Stress can be defined in terms of the body's response to a threatening event or to something in the environment that produces this response.

EXPANSION

- Stress can also be seen as the lack of fit between the perceived demands of the environment and the perceived ability to cope.

THE HYPOTHALAMIC-PITUITARY-ADRENAL CORTEX PATHWAY (6-mark version)

1 This pathway is activated when higher brain centres evaluate a situation as stressful.

2 These higher brain centres instruct the hypothalamus to release corticotrophin releasing factor (CRF), which travels to the pituitary gland.

Okay to just use abbreviations 'CRF' and 'ACTH' here!

3 CRF causes the pituitary gland to release adrenocorticotrophic hormone (ACTH) into the bloodstream.

4 ACTH travels to the adrenal cortex and stimulates the release of corticosteroids into the bloodstream.

5 These corticosteroids have a variety of effects throughout the body and form part of the stress response.

A 3-MARK VERSION

- When the brain evaluates a situation as stressful, the hypothalamus sends a message to the pituitary gland to release ACTH into the bloodstream.
- ACTH in turn prompts the adrenal cortex to create corticosteroids, which have a variety of effects as part of the body's response to a stressor.

THE HYPOTHALAMIC-AUTONOMIC NERVOUS SYSTEM-ADRENAL MEDULLA PATHWAY (6-mark version)

1 In response to stressors or to danger, the adrenal medulla is activated by the sympathetic branch of the ANS.

2 The adrenal medulla releases adrenaline and noradrenaline into the bloodstream.

3 These hormones reinforce the activating effect of the sympathetic nervous system, preparing the body for flight or fight.

4 Adrenaline prepares the body for flight and the noradrenaline prepares the body for fight.

5 Effects include increased heart rate and blood pressure, and the further mobilisation of energy reserves.

A 3-MARK VERSION

- The ANS activates the adrenal medulla, which releases adrenaline and noradrenaline into the bloodstream.
- These hormones support the action of the sympathetic branch of the ANS, preparing the body for a flight or fight response.

PHYSIOLOGY OF THE STRESS RESPONSE

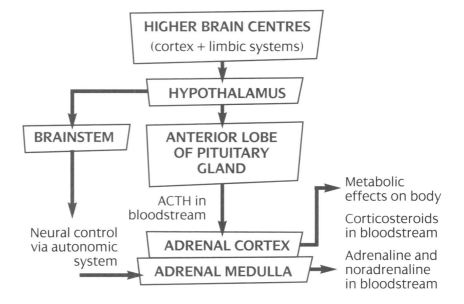

DEFINITION

The general adaptation syndrome is a stage model of how the body reacts during stressful situations. The three stages are alarm, resistance and exhaustion.

MUST REMEMBER...
To put these three stages in the right order. Could use the acronym **ARE**.

THE GENERAL ADAPTATION SYNDROME
(6-mark version)

1 In the **alarm stage**, the presence of a stressful event is registered and an arousal response is activated. The body is prepared to respond to the threat posed by the stressful event.

2 In the **resistance stage**, the stress response is fully activated. From the outside, things appear to be back under control, but resources are gradually being depleted.

3 If the stressor is long-lasting, the body enters the **exhaustion stage**. Hormone reserves are now exhausted and the body is vulnerable to stress-related illnesses such as ulcers and depression.

A 3-MARK VERSION

1 In the **alarm stage**, an arousal response is activated.

2 In the **resistance stage**, the stress response is fully activated and apparently coping with the stressor.

3 In the **exhaustion stage**, hormone reserves are exhausted and the body is vulnerable to stress-related illnesses.

Could draw some conclusions from this research and then use these as AO2 material for the AO1 + AO2 question.

THE THREE STAGES OF SELYE'S GENERAL ADAPTATION SYNDROME

PHASE 1: ALARM
Stress response – systems activated

▼

PHASE 2: RESISTANCE
Body copes with stress

▼

PHASE 3: EXHAUSTION
Stress-related illness may develop

CRITICISMS OF THE GENERAL ADAPTATION SYNDROME

Use of animals
- The GAS model was based on research with non-human animals using physical stressors.
- However, humans respond mostly to psychological stressors, relying more on cognitive processes to deal with these.
- This makes it difficult to generalise these research findings to humans.

Individual differences
- The GAS ignores individual differences such as Type A behaviour and gender.
- It assumes that everybody responds in the same way to stressors.
- However, research has shown that personality and gender affect stress reactions.

TYPICAL QUESTIONS...

AO1 QUESTIONS

1 What is meant by 'stress'? (2 marks)

2 Explain what is meant by 'stress'. (3 marks)

3 Explain what is meant by the 'general adaptation syndrome'. (3 marks)

4 Outline two ways in which the body responds to stressors. (3 + 3 marks)

5 Describe one way in which the body responds to stressors. (6 marks)

6 Describe the main features of the general adaptation syndrome. (6 marks)

7 Give two criticisms of the general adaptation syndrome. (3 + 3 marks)

8 Outline the general adaptation syndrome and give one criticism of this syndrome. (3 + 3 marks)

AO1 + AO2 QUESTION

9 Outline and evaluate one or more ways in which the body responds to stressors. (18 marks)

STRESS AND CARDIOVASCULAR DISORDERS

DEFINITION

Cardiovascular disorders are any disorder of the cardiovascular system, which is responsible for distributing oxygen and nutrients to the body's organs.

EXPANSION

• These include high blood pressure, coronary heart disease or stroke.

SOME EFFECTS OF STRESS ON THE CARDIOVASCULAR SYSTEM

Hypertension
Raised blood pressure caused by furring up of blood vessels.

Atherosclerosis
Raised blood pressure wears away the lining of blood vessels. Scarring of these blood vessels then acts as a collection point for circulating fats. Plaques form and these gradually block blood vessels.

Stroke
Caused by plaques blocking the blood vessels in the brain.

Coronary heart disease
Caused by damage to the functioning of the heart which is responsible for pumping blood around the body.

*These are **not** required but can be used to illustrate answers to questions in this area.*

MUST TAKE CARE ...
To use a study that **specifically** investigates stress and cardiovascular disorders rather than just stress and illness.

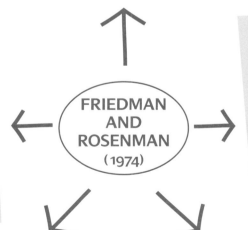

Aims
To investigate links between Type A behaviour patterns and cardiovascular disease. Specifically the study tested the hypothesis that Type A individuals are more likely to develop coronary heart disease than Type B individuals.

Procedures
• Using structured interviews, 3,200 men aged 39–59 were categorised as either Type A, Type B or Type X (balanced between Type A and Type B).
• Assessment based on answers to interview questions and behaviour during the interview.
• All the men were free from coronary heart disease at the start of the research.
• The sample was followed up for 8½ years to assess lifestyle and health outcomes.

FRIEDMAN AND ROSENMAN (1974)

Findings
• At the end of the study, 257 of the men had developed coronary heart disease.
• 70% of these were from the Type A group, twice the rate found in the Type B group.
• This association was significant even when risk factors such as smoking and obesity were taken into account.

Conclusions
• The Type A behaviour pattern was found to be an independent risk factor for heart disease increasing vulnerability far more than the Type B behaviour pattern.
• Behaviour modification programmes to reduce Type A behaviour should thus result in a reduced risk of heart disease.

Criticism
• This wasn't an experimental study, so cause and effect couldn't be established. Other studies have failed to show a relationship between Type A behaviour and heart disease.

OTHER FINDINGS OF RESEARCH INTO STRESS AND CARDIOVASCULAR DISORDERS

Steenland et al. (1997)
The relationship between job strain and heart disease was evaluated in a study of US blue collar workers. Two factors were assessed: job control and job demand. Workers in high control and high demand jobs had a significantly decreased risk of heart disease compared with other workers.

Sheps et al. (1999)
They gave men and women a variety of physical and psychological tests, designed to put them under mental stress. Those who had **ischemia** displayed an erratic heartbeat during the test, and were more likely to die three to four years later.

Möller et al. (2005)
They monitored the number of first heart attacks in a study of over 3,500 people aged between 45 and 70. They found that women were three times as likely, and men six times as likely to have a heart attack if they had taken on increased responsibilities at work.

> Ischemia – reduction of blood flow to the heart.

OTHER CONCLUSIONS OF RESEARCH INTO STRESS AND CARDIOVASCULAR DISORDERS

- Steenland et al. concluded that there was no evidence of an increased risk of heart disease for those with high demand jobs. However, those with the highest job control appeared to have a significantly decreased risk of heart disease.

- Sheps et al. concluded that patients with **ischemia** may not die suddenly while under conditions of mental stress, but are more likely to succumb to heart disease later.

- Möller et al. concluded that work stress was a significant risk factor for heart attacks, particularly where participants felt affected by work conflict, or where they perceived extra responsibilities to be stressful.

EVALUATION OF RESEARCH INTO STRESS AND CARDIOVASCULAR DISORDERS

Criticisms

- **Uncontrolled variables**: many of the studies of stress and cardiovascular disorders have failed to control for other aspects of lifestyle that might have affected vulnerability to heart disease (e.g. hardiness or cultural background).

- **Stress as an independent risk factor**: we don't know if stress acts as an independent risk factor for cardiovascular disease. Stress may lead to other risk factors, such as smoking, physical inactivity and overeating, which then lead to heart disease.

- **Control rather than demand**: a number of studies (e.g. Steenland et al., 1997) have shown that traditional risk factors for heart disease (e.g. job demand), are less important than control.

> In an AO1 + AO2 question, findings can be used as AO1 and conclusions as AO2.

TYPICAL QUESTIONS...

AO1 QUESTIONS

1 What is meant by 'cardiovascular disorders'? (2 marks)

2 Explain what is meant by 'cardiovascular disorders'. (3 marks)

3 Outline findings of research into stress and cardiovascular disorders. (6 marks)

4 Outline conclusions of research into stress and cardiovascular disorders. (6 marks)

5 Describe the aims and procedures of one study of stress and cardiovascular disorders. (6 marks)

6 Describe the findings and conclusions of one study of stress and cardiovascular disorders. (6 marks)

7 Describe the aims and conclusions of one study of stress and cardiovascular disorders. (6 marks)

8 Describe the findings and give one criticism of one study of stress and cardiovascular disorders. (6 marks)

9 Give two criticisms of research into stress and cardiovascular disorders. (3 + 3 marks)

AO1 + AO2 QUESTION

10 Outline and evaluate research into the relationship between stress and cardiovascular disorders. (18 marks)

> **MUST REMEMBER...**
> That 'APFCC' questions can be any combination of aims, procedures, criticisms, etc.

STRESS AND THE IMMUNE SYSTEM

DEFINITION

The immune system refers to the system that protects the body against infection. It is a network of cells and chemicals that seek out and destroy invading particles.

EXPANSION

- Research has found that stress can **reduce immune system functioning** by reducing the concentration of cytokines, which help to ward off infections.

SOME EFFECTS OF STRESS ON THE IMMUNE SYSTEM

Infection and diseases

Stress causes physiological changes that tend to weaken our immune system. As a result, our health can be negatively affected: infections and illness occur more frequently and recovery takes longer.

Indirect effects

Stress causes the release of ACTH from the pituitary gland in the brain which signals the adrenal glands to release anti-inflammatory hormones. These inhibit immune cell functioning.

Psoriasis and eczema

Symptoms of inflammatory disorders such as psoriasis and eczema worsen with stress. Stress interferes with the immune system's ability to deal with the inflammation associated with these disorders.

Although these are not attributable to one researcher, they still count as research **findings.**

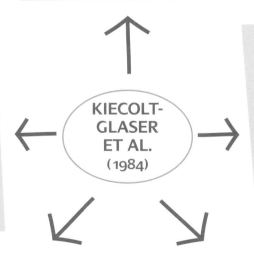

Aims

To investigate whether the stress of important examinations has an effect on immune system functioning. Specifically this was to see whether relatively short-term, predictable stressors can increase vulnerability to illness.

Procedures

- This was a natural experiment using 75 medical students.
- Blood samples were taken one month before the exam (low stress) and during the exam period (high stress).
- Immune system functioning was assessed by measuring NK cell activity in the blood samples.
- Students were also given questionnaires to assess psychological variables such as life events.

KIECOLT-GLASER ET AL. (1984)

Findings

- NK cell activity was significantly reduced in the second blood sample taken during the exams compared to the sample taken one month before.
- NK cell activity was also reduced in participants reporting other significant life stressors, and in those who were anxious and depressed.

Conclusions

- Short-term, predictable stressors reduce immune system functioning, increasing vulnerability to illness and infection.
- Immune system functioning is also affected by psychological variables (such as life events) which make individuals more vulnerable to the added effects of short-term stressors.

Criticism

- This study was carried out on students, who may be a special group, therefore generalisations must be made with caution. However the results *are* in line with studies of other groups, e.g. women going through divorce and carers of Alzheimer's disease patients.

OTHER FINDINGS OF RESEARCH INTO STRESS AND THE IMMUNE SYSTEM

Sapolsky (1992)
Sapolsky has shown that stress, such as strenuous exercise or cold exposure, can suppress the immune system.

Kiecolt-Glaser et al. (1995)
The amount of time it took for a wound to heal was found to be significantly longer in a stressed group of Alzheimer's carers compared to a control group.

Andersen (1998)
Breast cancer patients who experienced high levels of stress concerning their diagnosis and treatment show evidence of a weakened immune system compared to patients experiencing less stress.

Cohen et al. (1993)
Participants who experienced a high degree of stress, measured by negative life events and the emotions associated with these, showed increased vulnerability to infection following exposure to the common cold virus.

OTHER CONCLUSIONS OF RESEARCH INTO STRESS AND THE IMMUNE SYSTEM

Sapolsky (1992)
This should mean that exercise, diet and social support can improve immune system function, which is what has been found to occur in later studies (Sapolsky, 1994).

Kiecolt-Glaser et al. (1995)
These findings support the view that chronic stress depresses the functioning of the immune system because wound healing was slower in a chronically stressed group.

Andersen (1998)
These results suggest that psychological stress may play a role in how the immune system responds to cancer.

Cohen et al. (1993)
This shows that high levels of stress reduce immune system function and make a person more vulnerable to viral infection.

These conclusions can be built into AO2 commentary.

EVALUATION OF RESEARCH INTO STRESS AND IMMUNE SYSTEM FUNCTIONING

Criticisms
- Correlational studies: many of these studies (e.g. Cohen et al., 1993) are correlational, so do not demonstrate a causal relationship between stress and immune system functioning. However, they strongly suggest that high levels of stress reduce immune function and make a person more vulnerable to illness.
- Intervention: if stress *reduces* immune system functioning, then reducing stress should *improve* it. This is what was found in a study which looked at the beneficial effects of exercise, diet and social support (Sapolsky, 1994).

Other commentary
- Gender differences: Kiecolt-Glaser (2003) claims there are significant differences between women and men in the way their immune system reacts to marital conflict, with women showing more adverse hormonal and immunological changes.
- Age differences: Segerstrom and Miller (2004) claims that age increases a person's vulnerability to stress-related decreases in immune function. Age makes it harder for the body to regulate itself.

TYPICAL QUESTIONS...

AO1 QUESTIONS

1 What is meant by the 'immune system'? (2 marks)

2 Explain what is meant by 'immune system'. (3 marks)

3 Outline findings of research into stress and the immune system. (6 marks)

4 Outline conclusions of research into stress and the immune system. (6 marks)

5 Describe the aims and procedures of one study of stress and the immune system. (6 marks)

6 Describe the findings and conclusions of one study of stress and the immune system. (6 marks)

7 Describe the aims and conclusions of one study of stress and the immune system. (6 marks)

8 Describe the findings and give one criticism of one study of stress and the immune system. (6 marks)

9 Give two criticisms of research into stress and the immune system. (3 + 3 marks)

AO1 +AO2 QUESTION

10 Outline and evaluate research into the relationship between stress and the immune system. (18 marks).

SOURCES OF STRESS: LIFE CHANGES

DEFINITION

Life changes are major events, such as marriage and divorce, that have a psychological impact on the individual.

EXPANSION
- These are used to investigate the relationship between life changes and stress-related illness.

HOW ARE LIFE EVENTS LINKED TO STRESS?

DIVORCE

Divorce causes stress for a variety of reasons. First, divorce creates higher stress levels between the two individuals, making them more susceptible to depression (Hines, 1997). Research also supports the notion that divorce negatively affects the immune system.

BEREAVEMENT

All types of bereavement tend to be perceived by the survivor as stressful, but traumatic deaths (e.g. sudden or violent deaths) are associated with separation distress (that comes with the death) and trauma distress (associated with *how* the person died).

These can be used independently (in a 3 + 3-mark question), or as research findings (for 6 AO1 marks).

MUST TAKE CARE...
To give only the parts of this study which are asked for in the question.

Aims
To investigate whether scores on the Holmes and Rahe Social Readjustment Rating Scale (SRRS) were correlated with the subsequent onset of illness.

Procedures
- SRRS given to 2,500 US sailors to assess how many life events experienced in previous 6 months.
- The total score on the SRRS was recorded for each participant.
- Over the next 6 months, detailed records were kept of the men's health status.
- Score on the SRRS was then correlated with the men's illness scores over that 6-month period.

Findings
- There was a positive correlation of + 0.118 between the SRRS score and illness scores.
- This was a small but significant correlation.
- As the number of life units increased (as measured by the SRRS), so did the frequency of illness over the subsequent 6 months.

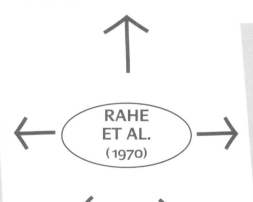

RAHE ET AL. (1970)

Conclusions
- Life change units are positively correlated with illness scores.
- Experiencing more life events increased the chance of stress-related health breakdown.
- As the correlation was not perfect (i.e. + 1), this suggests life events were not the only factors contributing to illness.

Criticism
- The correlation between life events and subsequent illness does not imply that the life events *caused* the illness. For example, depressed or anxious people may bring about more negative events such as divorce rather than the other around.

OTHER FINDINGS OF RESEARCH INTO THE RELATIONSHIP BETWEEN LIFE CHANGES AND STRESS

Glaser et al. (1987)
Researchers followed students through the academic year and compared the numbers of infectious illnesses during exam periods with non-exam periods. They found more evidence of illnesses during the exam periods.

Stone et al. (1987)
Married couples completed daily checklists of events over a 3-month period. The number of undesirable events that they experienced increased 3 to 4 days prior to the onset of illness, and desirable events decreased during the same period.

OTHER CONCLUSIONS OF RESEARCH INTO THE RELATIONSHIP BETWEEN LIFE CHANGES AND STRESS

Glaser et al. (1987)
This suggests that people who are stressed by short-term and relatively minor life events are slower to develop an antibody response to infections, and could also be at greater risk of developing more severe illness.

Stone et al. (1987)
Because a sequence of undesirable events preceded the onset of illness, this suggests that they might have been responsible for the stress-related illness. This is supported by the fact that the incidence of desirable events (which might buffer the individual from illness) decreased during the same period.

MUST TAKE CARE...
Not to confuse **findings** with **conclusions**.

EVALUATION OF RESEARCH INTO LIFE CHANGES AND STRESS

- **Other factors**: for many people the impact of life events such as divorce carries additional problems such as increased financial worries and the stress of single parenting. This means that it may not be the life event itself, but **life after the event** that contributes to stress-related illnesses such as depression.

- **Biased retrospective reports**: most studies have used only retrospective reports of major life events as a measure of stress. Research has shown that many people have a **tendency to remember more negative events** when depressed.

- **Diathesis-stress model**: the majority of stressful life events do not invariably trigger mental disorders. People are more likely to develop mental disorders such as depression as a result of negative life events if they are already **vulnerable biologically, socially or psychologically**.

- **Daily hassles**: the potential role of **minor life events** has largely been ignored. Minor stressors (hassles), which occur on a daily basis, appear to have a greater effect on stress-related illness (Hills and Norvell, 1991).

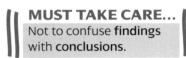

TYPICAL QUESTIONS...

AO1 QUESTIONS

1 What is meant by 'life changes? (2 marks)

2 Explain what is meant by 'life changes'. (3 marks)

3 Outline findings of research into life changes as a source of stress. (6 marks)

4 Outline conclusions of research into life changes as a source of stress. (6 marks)

5 Describe the aims and findings of one study that has investigated life changes as a source of stress. (6 marks)

6 Describe the procedures and conclusions of one study that has investigated life changes as a source of stress. (6 marks)

7 Describe the findings and conclusions of one study that has investigated life changes as a source of stress. (6 marks)

8 Describe the conclusions and give one criticism of one study that has investigated life changes as a source of stress. (6 marks)

9 Give two criticisms of research into life changes as a source of stress. (3 + 3 marks)

AO1 + AO2 QUESTION

10 Consider the claim that life changes are a significant source of stress. (18 marks)

SOURCES OF STRESS: WORKPLACE STRESSORS

MUST KNOW...
- Research into the effects of the workplace as a source of stress.

DEFINITION

Workplace stressors are aspects of the workplace environment which we experience as stressful and which lead to a stress response.

EXPANSION
- These include physical stressors, such as noise and heat, and psychological stressors, such as lack of control.

HOW ARE WORKPLACE STRESSORS LINKED TO STRESS?

THE PHYSICAL ENVIRONMENT

Physical stressors such as noise and heat make work more difficult and more energy has to be expended to overcome them. The increased arousal can lead to frustration and a number of studies have shown that increased temperature and exposure to intense noise can lead to stress and aggression.

LACK OF CONTROL

In many organisations, other people often determine workload and work patterns. Research with humans and animals has shown that a perceived lack of control increases the stress-response and contributes to stress and illness.

It's a good idea to use bullet points when revising this material.

MUST REMEMBER...
That research shows it is **perceived** lack of control that's important rather than actual lack of control.

Aims
To investigate whether work stressors (such as repetitiveness and high levels of responsibility) increase stress-related physiological arousal and stress-related illness.

Procedures
- Researchers identified high-risk group of 14 'finishers' who finished off wood in a Swedish sawmill.
- Work was machine-paced, repetitive but highly skilled, and their productivity determined wage rates for whole factory.
- Compared with low-risk group of 10 cleaners whose work was more varied and self-paced.
- Levels of stress-related hormones measured on work days and rest days.
- Records were kept of stress-related illness and absenteeism.

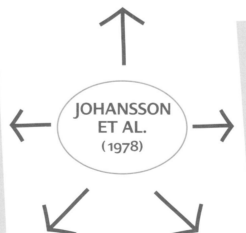

JOHANSSON ET AL. (1978)

Findings
- High-risk group of finishers secreted more stress hormones on work days than on rest days, and higher levels than the control group.
- The finishers also showed significantly higher levels of stress-related illness (such as headaches) and absenteeism than the low-risk group of cleaners.

Conclusions
- A combination of stressors, especially repetitiveness, machine pacing of work and high levels of responsibility leads to long-term physiological arousal. This in turn leads to stress-related illness and absenteeism.
- To reduce illness and absenteeism, employers would need to find ways of reducing these work stressors, e.g. by having control over the pace of their work.

Criticism
- The study does not identify which of the various work stressors might be the most stressful. The high-risk group was exposed to a number of different stressors. To separate out the effects of each of these different factors, a more controlled experimental study would be necessary.

OTHER FINDINGS OF RESEARCH INTO WORKPLACE STRESSORS

Marmot et al. (1991)
They measured job control and stress-related illness among civil servants. They found that people with low job control were much more likely to die of a heart attack than those with high job control.

Schaubroeck et al. (2001)
Having high levels of control in a job can be stressful for some people. Schaubroeck et al. found that employees who perceived they had control over their job responsibilities but didn't have confidence in their ability to handle the demands of the role or who blamed themselves for negative outcomes were more likely to experience the most stress.

OTHER CONCLUSIONS OF RESEARCH INTO WORKPLACE STRESSORS

Marmot et al. (1991)
They concluded that a combination of high job demands and low control is associated with an increased chance of heart disease.

Schaubroeck et al. (2001)
This research shows that increasing job control can be harmful for individuals who lack the capacity to handle it or when this control increases their self-blame when things go wrong.

These conclusions can be built into AO2 commentary.

MUST REMEMBER...
That the Johansson et al. study can also contribute to answers on research findings and/or conclusions.

EVALUATION OF RESEARCH INTO WORKPLACE STRESS

Criticisms
• **Individual differences**: some important variables, such as personality, were not controlled for in these studies. It is possible (e.g. in Marmot et al.'s study of civil servants) that people with Type A personality are attracted to stressful jobs, and it is this which causes health problems.

• **Research support**: research has shown that as other cultures (e.g. in eastern Europe) take on the working practices of the West, a similar relationship between lack of control and stress-related illness is becoming evident.

Other commentary
• **Job control**: researchers have generally found that lack of job control is a significant determinant of stress, but some research studies (e.g. Schaubroeck et al., 2001) have shown that this is not true for all people. Some people find it *more* stressful to have control, and that increased levels of control lead to increased stress levels.

• **The cost of workplace stress**: the cost of stress in the workplace is demonstrated by lowered productivity and excessive absenteeism, as well as premature loss of key workers who develop stress-related health problems.

TYPICAL QUESTIONS...

AO1 QUESTIONS

1 What is meant by 'stress', 'stressors' and 'workplace stressors'? (2 + 2 + 2 marks)

2 Explain what is meant by 'workplace stressors'. (3 marks)

3 Describe two ways in which the workplace may be a source of stress. (3 + 3 marks)

4 Outline findings of research into the the effect of workplace stressors. (6 marks)

5 Outline conclusions of research into the effect of workplace stressors. (6 marks)

6 Describe the aims and findings of one study that has investigated workplace stressors. (6 marks)

7 Describe the procedures and conclusions of one study of stress and the immune system. (6 marks)

8 Describe the findings of one study that has investigated workplace stressors and give one criticism of this study. (6 marks)

9 Give two criticisms of research into the effects of workplace stressors. (3 + 3 marks)

AO1 + AO2 QUESTION

10 To what extent is the workplace a significant source of stress? (18 marks)

INDIVIDUAL DIFFERENCES AND STRESS: PERSONALITY

HOW DOES PERSONALITY MODIFY THE EFFECTS OF STRESS?

TYPE A BEHAVIOUR

Friedman and Rosenman (1974) proposed that a particular behaviour pattern was associated with increased vulnerability to coronary heart disease (CHD). This Type A behaviour pattern is characterised by constant time pressure, competitiveness in work and social situations, and anger, i.e. being easily frustrated by the efforts of others.

THE HARDY PERSONALITY

Kobasa and Maddi (1977) proposed the idea of hardiness. Hardiness includes a range of personality characteristics, which if present provide defences against the negative effects of stress. These are control over what happens in ones life, commitment (i.e. a sense of involvement in the world), and challenge (i.e. life changes are opportunities rather than threats).

RESEARCH EVIDENCE FOR TYPE A

Friedman and Rosenman (1974)
They found that twice as many Type A men in their sample developed CHD over a 8½ year period compared to Type B men. This difference was independent of other factors known to increase chances of heart disease.

Myrtek (2001)
Carried out a meta-analysis of studies in this area, and found an association between CHD and a component of Type A personality – hostility. Other than this, there was no evidence of an association between Type A personality and CHD.

TYPE B AND TYPE C

- People with Type B personalities are better at relaxing without feeling guilty, are more relaxed about time, and are not easily angered.
- Type C people do not express negative emotions easily so that when they are angry they tend to bottle up the emotion. The incidence of cancer is significantly higher among Type C personalities.
- Whereas Type A and Type C expose the person to heart attack and cancer respectively, the Type B disposition avoids such fatal diseases.

RESEARCH EVIDENCE FOR THE HARDY PERSONALITY

Maddi et al.
Maddi et al. studied employees of a US company that was dramatically reducing the size of its workforce over one year. Two-thirds of employees suffered stress-related illness over the period, but the remaining one-third thrived. These showed more evidence of hardiness attitudes, i.e. commitment, control and challenge.

Bartone (1999)
Hardiness protected US Army personnel in the Gulf War in the 1990's. The higher the hardiness level, the greater the ability of soldiers to experience combat-related stress without negative health consequences, such as post traumatic stress disorder or depression.

TYPE A BEHAVIOUR PATTERN

TIME PRESSURE
- Working against the clock.
- Doing several things at once.
- Irritation and impatience with others.
- Unhappy doing nothing.

COMPETITIVENESS
- Always plays to win at games and at work.
- Achievement measured as material productivity.

ANGER
- Self-critical.
- Hostile to the outside world.
- Anger often directed inwards.

The role of hostility
Later research has shown that the critical personality variable in this relationship is hostility. When high levels of repressed hostility are combined with high levels of Type A behaviour, correlations with CHD are significantly increased (Matthews and Haynes, 1986).

Lack of consistent research support
Many studies have looked at the relationship between the Type A personality and CHD. Correlations tend not to be high, and a number of studies have reported negative findings. This has led some (e.g. Evans, 1990) to question the value of the Type A concept.

Protective factors
Although Type A behaviours such as haste, time pressure and hostility may make the individual more vulnerable to CHD, they may also score high on other factors which protect them from CHD (e.g. use of physical exercise and presence of social support).

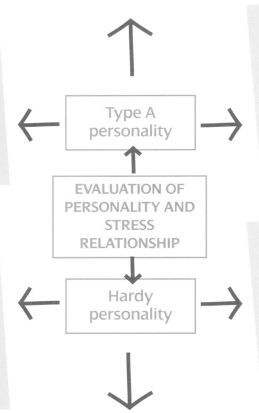

Type A personality

EVALUATION OF PERSONALITY AND STRESS RELATIONSHIP

Hardy personality

Type A and hardiness
Although Type A behaviour is claimed to be a risk for CHD, many Type A individuals appear resistant to heart disease. This may be because they also possess aspects of the hardy personality (commitment, control, etc.), which would help them be resistant to the damaging effects of stress.

Participants
Much of the research in this area has been carried out on male executives or male soldiers. Results may not be generalisable to other groups or to women, as other research shows that gender has a significant effect on modifying the effects of stressors.

MUST REMEMBER...
That all of this could be used as AO2, but need to be selective rather than trying to get it all in!

Components of personality
The components of the hardy personality have never been very clearly defined — control may be an important part of commitment and challenge rather than being a separate factor. It is possible that researchers have simply shown the importance of control in protecting against the effects of stress rather than providing evidence for a full personality type .

For practice in answering AS Psychology questions, why not use *Collins Exam Practice AS Psychology*?

TYPICAL QUESTIONS...

AO1 QUESTIONS

1 Outline two ways in which personality might modify the effects of stressors. (3 + 3 marks)

2 Outline two ways in which individual differences might modify the effects of stressors. (3 + 3 marks)

3 Outline findings of research into how personality might modify the effects of stressors. (6 marks)

4 Outline conclusions of research into how personality might modify the effects of stressors. (6 marks)

AO1 + AO2 QUESTIONS

5 To what extent does personality modify the effects of stressors? (18 marks)

6 Outline and evaluate two ways in which personality might modify the effects of stressors. (18 marks)

The same answer could be used for both questions if restricted to two ways.

INDIVIDUAL DIFFERENCES AND STRESS: GENDER

These are the 'two ways' needed to answer a '3 + 3' question.

HOW DOES GENDER MODIFY THE EFFECTS OF STRESS?

PHYSIOLOGICAL REACTIVITY

Frankenhaeuser et al. (1976) measured levels of stress hormones in boys and girls taking an exam. Boys showed a more rapid increase in hormone levels which took longer to return to normal. The girls' increase was slower and smaller and returned to normal more quickly.

GENDER DIFFERENCES IN COPING

Stone and Neale (1984) showed that men engage in direct action in coping with stressful events, whereas women are more likely to make use of relaxation techniques and social support. Women tend to use more passive strategies in dealing with stress, whereas men engage in more active coping strategies.

RESEARCH EVIDENCE FOR GENDER DIFFERENCES IN REACTIVITY

Stoney et al. (1990) Found that women showed smaller rises in blood pressure during stressful tasks than did men. In a later study (1991), a hypothesis that the gender relevance of a stressor determined the level of physiological response was not supported.

Kudielka et al. (2004) Found that a heightened HPA response pattern in young men decreases with age, resulting in similar responses in elderly men and women.

EXPLAINING GENDER DIFFERENCES IN REACTIVITY

• The hypothalamus-pituitary and ANS stress pathways may be more reactive in men than in women.

• Men and women vary in their attitude to stressful tasks, and this difference influences the stress response.

• Women's bodies produce oxytocin, which has a calming effect during stress. In contrast, men produce high levels of testosterone during stress, which causes hostility and withdrawal.

This can be used as AO2 evaluation.

EXPLAINING GENDER DIFFERENCES IN COPING

Socialisation theory (Pearlin and Schooler, 1978)
Women are taught to express their emotions more openly and to act in a more passive manner. Men, on the other hand, are taught to deal with situations in a more active and problem-focused manner.

Tend and befriend response (Taylor et al. (2000)
Women are likely to seek social contact to deal with stress, rather than showing a 'fight-or-flight' response. Females respond to stressful conditions by protecting and nurturing their young, and by seeking social contact and support from other females.

RESEARCH EVIDENCE FOR GENDER DIFFERENCES IN COPING

Billings and Moos (1981)
Found that men used more problem-focused coping whereas women used more emotion-focused and avoidance coping.

Tamres et al. (2002) Carried out a meta-analysis and found that women were more likely to seek emotional support, think over problems, and use positive self-talk. Other sex differences were dependent on the nature of the stressor.

Why is it important to know about gender differences?
This may also help researchers understand why men are more vulnerable to the negative health effects of stress (such as CHD). This may be because the 'tend and befriend' response may actually protect women against the adverse effects of stress whereas the 'fight or flight' response makes men more vulnerable to cardiovascular disorders.

Lack of consistent research support
Research has failed to find consistent gender differences in coping strategy use. For example, Rosario et al. (1988) found in three studies that men and women in the same social roles did not differ in their use of problem-focused or emotion-focused coping strategy use.

Oxytocin
The 'tend and befriend' response to stress may be due to the hormone oxytocin. This is produced by both sexes when faced with stress, but its effects are reinforced by the female hormone oestrogen and inhibited by male hormones. People with high levels of oxytocin tend to be more relaxed and less anxious.

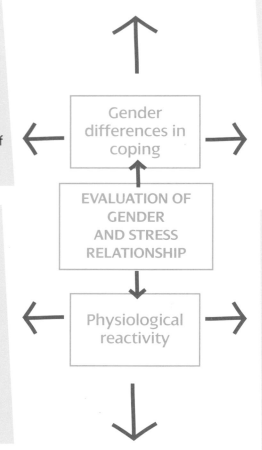

Gender differences in coping

EVALUATION OF GENDER AND STRESS RELATIONSHIP

Physiological reactivity

Lack of consistent research support
A number of studies (e.g. Sato et al., 2003) have failed to find evidence of gender differences in physiological reactivity when participants carried out stressful tasks. Other studies (e.g. Evans and Steptoe, 2003) have discovered that physiological stress reactions in men and women are greater when the demands of a task are not congruent with gender-related preferred modes of behaviour.

Does the gender gap still exist?
In 1998, the proportion of males in the UK who received treatment for CHD was 70% higher than for females. However, research (e.g. Rosenfeld, 2001) suggests that the gender gap in CHD is steadily decreasing and that this may be due to the increasing competitive pressure placed on women in the workplace and the changing nature of the female role.

MUST TAKE CARE...
To always **use** this material in an AO2 way, e.g. 'The claim that gender differences in coping exist is supported by...'

Research support
Holt-Lunstad et al. (2001) found that both sexes showed higher diastolic blood pressure (DBP) reactivity when competing against someone from the opposite sex in a work situation. Men showed greater DBP reactivity when losing than when winning, but women demonstrated the opposite pattern. This shows that gender differences may play an important role in how people respond to stressful interpersonal situations.

TYPICAL QUESTIONS...

AO1 QUESTIONS

1 Outline two ways in which gender might modify the effects of stressors. (3 + 3 marks)

2 Outline how gender and personality might modify the effects of stressors. (3 + 3 marks)

3 Outline findings of research into how gender might modify the effects of stressors. (6 marks)

4 Outline conclusions of research into how gender might modify the effects of stressors. (6 marks)

AO1 + AO2 QUESTIONS

5 To what extent does gender modify the effects of stressors? (18 marks)

6 Outline and evaluate two ways in which gender might modify the effects of stressors. (18 marks)

PHYSIOLOGICAL METHODS OF STRESS MANAGEMENT

MUST KNOW...
• Two physiological methods of stress management and their strengths and weaknesses.

The physiological approach to stress management involves the use of drugs and/or biofeedback to target directly the stress-response systems themselves.

MUST REMEMBER...
To write about at least two types of drugs (e.g. BZs and beta-blockers).

DRUGS

Benzodiazepines (BZs) – often used for the short-term relief of severe anxiety.

Beta-blockers – used in the treatment of high blood pressure (hypertension).

HOW DO THEY WORK?

1 BZs work by enhancing the actions of a natural brain chemical, GABA.
2 GABA tells the neurons that it contacts to slow down or stop firing. This means that it has a general quietening influence on the brain.
3 This action of GABA is supported by BZs which thus exert an extra inhibitory influence on neurons.
4 As a result of this extra influence, the brain's output of excitatory neurotransmitters is reduced and the person feels calmer.

HOW DO THEY WORK?

1 Beta-blockers work by reducing the activity of adrenaline and noradrenaline, which are key agents in sympathetic arousal.
2 By blocking sympathetic arousal, beta-blockers slow the heart beat, lessen the force with which the heart contracts and reduces blood vessel contraction.
3 This results in a fall in blood pressure and less stress on the heart.

EVALUATION OF DRUGS AS A FORM OF STRESS MANAGEMENT

Strengths
• The major advantages of BZs are **high efficacy** (they are effective in the treatment of several different anxiety disorders), **rapid onset of action** (they work quickly, rapidly reducing the disabling effects of stress-related anxiety) and **low toxicity**.
• Beta-blockers can benefit patients with certain serious heart problems. Rai et al. (2005) found that beta-blockers **increased patients' survival**, independent of their age and gender.
• Drugs can be prescribed immediately, therefore are a **rapid form of intervention** in acute stress-related conditions.

Weaknesses
• BZs are often prescribed for acute stress-related reactions, e.g. bereavement. Although they may provide temporary relief from distress, if used for more than a few days they can **prevent normal psychological adjustment** to such trauma.
• Benzodiazepines are potentially addictive drugs: psychological and physical dependence can develop within a few weeks of repeated use.
• Many drugs have **side effects**. Beta-blockers can cause dizziness, sleep problems and decreased sexual ability in men.
• Some studies have found an increased **risk of developing diabetes** in people who take beta blockers.

MUST TAKE CARE...
To cover strengths **and** weaknesses when evaluating drugs as a form of stress management.

BIOFEEDBACK

- Biofeedback involves recording the activity of the **physiological systems** of the body's stress response.
- These include heart rate and blood pressure.
- Recording is made **via electrodes** on the skin that lead to a monitor.
- People try various strategies to reduce the physiological readings from these systems.
- Once a strategy is found which works consistently, it can be transferred to situations outside the laboratory.

HOW DOES IT WORK?

Physiological signals recorded, e.g. blood pressure, muscle tension — Recording of stress-related physiological effects

Signals amplified and displayed to client on a screen or via headphones — Biofeedback to client

Client uses relaxation, imagery, etc., to reduce blood pressure or muscle tension — Use of psychological stress management techniques

EVALUATION OF BIOFEEDBACK

Strengths
- **Biofeedback is a non-invasive treatment**, i.e. although the treatment involves manipulation of bodily processes such as heart rate and brain-wave activity, this occurs without penetrating the body.
- Biofeedback **does not have the side effects** associated with drugs, therefore is the treatment of choice for people who want to reduce or to stop taking drug medications.

Weaknesses
- Biofeedback is often found to be **no more effective than relaxation procedures**. This suggests that feedback on physiological processes is less important than relaxation in stress reduction.
- Biofeedback is **relatively expensive** in terms of equipment and time. If relaxation is the more important feature, the cost of the equipment could be avoided and training time reduced.

TYPICAL QUESTIONS...

AO1 QUESTIONS

1 What is meant by the 'physiological approach to stress management'? (2 marks)

2 Explain what is meant by 'physiological approach to stress management'. (3 marks)

3 Outline two physiological approaches to stress management. (3 + 3 marks)

4 Describe one physiological approach (e.g. drugs, biofeedback) to stress management. (6 marks)

5 Outline one physiological approach to stress management and give one strength of this approach. (3 + 3 marks)

6 Outline one physiological approach to stress management and give one criticism of this approach. (3 + 3 marks)

This could be the same answer as Q5 or could give a weakness.

7 Give one strength and one weakness of one physiological approach to stress management. (3 + 3 marks)

AO1 + AO2 QUESTIONS

8 Outline and evaluate two physiological methods of stress management. (18 marks)

9 Outline the physiological approach to stress management, and evaluate this approach in terms of its strengths and weaknesses. (18 marks)

PSYCHOLOGICAL METHODS OF STRESS MANAGEMENT

Psychological approaches to stress management involve the use of techniques that help people cope better with stressful situations or alter their perceptions of the demands of a stressful situation.

STRESS-INOCULATION TRAINING (SIT) (MEICHENBAUM AND CAMERON, 1983)	INCREASING HARDINESS (KOBASA AND MADDI, 1977)
SIT is a form of cognitive-behavioural therapy which attempts to increase an individual's ability to cope and to help them use already existing coping skills. It is used in a preventative way to 'inoculate' individuals against future stressors.	Hardiness training involves an assessment of how much stress a person is experiencing and how hardy their attitudes are, followed by training designed to teach people how to cope with stress, seek social support and relax.

Stage 1 – Conceptualisation

- Clients are encouraged to relive stressful situations and to analyse different features of the situation, such as 'how did they attempt to cope?' and 'why wasn't it successful?'
- Through this they are helped to gain a greater understanding of the nature of stress and their reactions to it.

Stage 2 – Skills training and practice

- Once the key elements of stressful situations have been identified, clients are taught specific strategies for coping with them.
- These might include relaxation techniques, increased control and social skills.

Stage 3 – Real-life application

- The final stage is for the client to go out into the real world and put their training to the test.
- The reinforcement of successful coping in the real world then becomes self-sustaining.

Stage 1 – Focusing

- Clients are trained and encouraged to spot signs of stress such as muscle tension and anxiety.
- This allows them to recognise stressful situations and so identify sources of stress.

Stage 2 – Reliving stressful encounters

- Clients analyse recent stressful situations in terms of how they were actually resolved, and how things might have turned out better or worse.
- This gives them an insight into their current coping strategies and how they might be more effective than they imagine.

Stage 3 – Self improvement

- Central to hardiness is the belief that we can cope with life's challenges.
- Clients must initially recognise and take on challenges that they *can* cope with before moving on to more complex problems.

EVALUATION OF PSYCHOLOGICAL METHODS

Strength
The combination of cognitive therapy (thinking about past situations and developing cognitive strategies) and behavioural therapy (training in new skills) makes stress-inoculation a powerful method of stress management.

Strength
By acquiring new skills, an individual can reduce the gap between demands and coping resources, and so gain more confidence to handle previously stressful situations.

Weakness
Clients must go through a rigorous programme over a long period, analysing responses to stress and learning new techniques. This requires high levels of motivation and commitment, so is not a quick fix.

STRESS-INOCULATION

Weakness
Any technique that aims to improve stress management may be acting against habits that are well established, even if they are not effective. Changing cognitions and behaviour will always be difficult.

Strength
Hardiness training has been effectively used by Olympic swimmers to ensure that they are committed to the challenge of increased performance levels, and are able to control stressful aspects of their daily lives that might otherwise interfere with their training (Fletcher, 2005).

MUST TAKE CARE...
When questions ask for strengths and weaknesses, then must give at least **two** strengths and **two** weaknesses

Strength
Several universities and colleges in the US offer hardiness training to their students. It has been effective with at-risk students and has helped them to master the many stresses they encounter while they work.

INCREASING HARDINESS

Weakness
Much of the research in this area has been carried out on a restricted sample of male executives or male soldiers within the US. Results may therefore not be generalisable to other cultural groups or to women.

Weakness
Hardiness training has the problem that it must address basic aspects of personality and learned habits of coping that are notoriously difficult to modify, therefore cannot be seen as a rapid solution to stress management.

TYPICAL QUESTIONS...

AO1 QUESTIONS

1 What is meant by the 'psychological approach to stress management'? (2 marks)

2 Explain what is meant by 'psychological approach to stress management'. (3 marks)

3 Outline two psychological approaches to stress management. (3 + 3 marks)

4 Describe one psychological approach (e.g. stress-inoculation, increasing hardiness) to stress management. (6 marks)

5 Outline one psychological approach to stress management and give one weakness of this approach. (3 + 3 marks)

6 Outline one psychological approach to stress management and give one criticism of this approach. (3 + 3 marks)

7 Give one strength and one weakness of one psychological approach to stress management. (3 + 3 marks)

AO1 + AO2 QUESTIONS

8 Outline and evaluate two psychological methods of stress management. (18 marks)

9 Outline the psychological approach to stress management, and evaluate this approach in terms of its strengths and weaknesses. (18 marks)

DEFINING PSYCHOLOGICAL ABNORMALITY (I)

DEFINITION

The definitions of abnormality are:
- statistical infrequency
- deviation from social norms
- deviation from ideal mental health
- failure to function adequately.

STATISTICAL INFREQUENCY

ASSUMPTIONS

- Behaviour is abnormal if it falls outside the range that is typical for most people, i.e. is statistically infrequent.
- Statisticians measure characteristics (IQ, traits like introversion, etc.) and then assess how these characteristics are distributed amongst the general population.
- One way of showing population distribution is by means of the normal distribution curve.
- The spread of scores is measured by the standard deviation (SD).
- Most scores are clustered round the middle, i.e. the mean.
- 68% of the population fall between one SD either side of the mean, and 95% between two SDs either side of the mean.
- It follows that scores outside this range are very unusual (i.e. 2.5% above it and 2.5% below it).

→

- One criterion for mental retardation, a psychological disorder, is an IQ score below 70, i.e. 2 SDs below the mean.

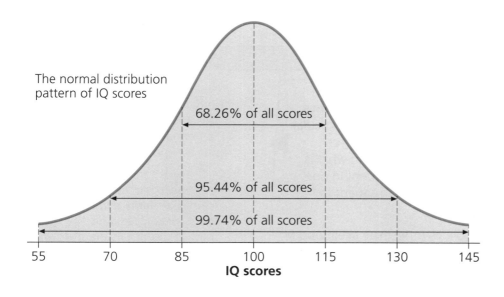

The normal distribution pattern of IQ scores

68.26% of all scores

95.44% of all scores

99.74% of all scores

55   70   85   100   115   130   145

IQ scores

LIMITATIONS ASSOCIATED WITH THE STATISTICAL INFREQUENCY DEFINITION

Which characteristics?

- Statistical infrequency definition is just a method for measuring abnormality. It does not suggest **which characteristics** might be related to abnormal behaviour.
- It does not discriminate between desirable and undesirable behaviours.

- e.g. Heroism and genius are statistically infrequent but are not seen as psychologically abnormal because they are desirable

Where to draw the line?

- It is difficult to decide where the **cut-off point** between normality and abnormality should be drawn.
- It is unlikely that abnormal states can be classified so strictly.

- e.g. Disorders like depression and anxiety have wide variations in severity.

What about common disorders?

- Certain states such as depression and anxiety are classified as abnormal because they interfere with normal functioning. However, they are **not particularly infrequent** statistically.

- e.g. Angst (1992) found that there is a one in ten chance of having a serious depressive episode at least once in your lifetime.

Statistics can be misleading

- Statistical infrequency can only be accurately calculated if complete data are available.
- Mental disorder statistics are only available for people who have been diagnosed. This could be **unrepresentative** because people suffering symptoms of mental disorders do not always seek professional help.

- Females are more likely to go to a doctor with anxiety problems than males. This could result in a distorted picture of the spread of the disorder.

Cultural issues

- The statistical infrequency definition is **culturally relative**, i.e. it only relates to a particular culture. Behaviours differ between cultures and what is statistically infrequent in one might be more frequent in another.
- Statistics reflect the likelihood of **seeking professional diagnosis** rather than the actual spread of particular disorders.

- e.g. In Puerto Rica, fainting fits and seizures are seen as a normal reaction to stress.

- e.g. In China, mental illness carries a stigma and so is rarely diagnosed. This probably conceals the true extent of mental problems within that particular culture.

DEFINING PSYCHOLOGICAL ABNORMALITY (2)

DEVIATION FROM SOCIAL NORMS

- **Explicit:** Highway Code in UK requires us to drive on the left.
- **Implicit:** Social convention requires us to sit silently during a play at the theatre.

ASSUMPTIONS
- Every society develops its own set of standards for acceptable behaviour (social norms).
- Rules about how to behave can be explicit or implicit.
- People who violate the rules are seen as deviant or abnormal.

- e.g. People with schizophrenia often show inappropriate emotions (crying at jokes or laughing at funerals, etc.). People with phobias often show bizarre behaviour when trying to escape the phobic object (leaving bags of shopping at the supermarket checkout, pushing people out of the way, etc.).

LIMITATIONS ASSOCIATED WITH THE DEVIATION FROM SOCIAL NORMS DEFINITION

Role of context
- Behaviour is context-specific.

- Wearing a bikini is acceptable on the beach but not in the classroom. Shouting 'Lovely bananas!' at passers-by is acceptable for a market trader but not for a shopper.

Change with the times
- Beliefs about morality and social norms change over time.
- In the UK, homosexual acts were criminal offences until 1967. In the USA, homosexuality was classified as a mental illness until 1973.

Abnormal or criminal?
- People who violate legal rules are usually seen as criminals rather than psychologically abnormal.
- However, it some cases, it can be difficult to differentiate.
- You would probably not see someone who had committed fraud as psychologically abnormal, but what about a serial rapist or murderer?

Cultural issues
- This definition is bound by culture because each culture defines its own set of social norms.
- Classification of mental disorders in the West is almost entirely based on middle-class, white culture. This is then applied to people from sub-cultures who live in the West where it might not be appropriate.
- This definition can be used as a form of social control.
- e.g. In the former Soviet Union, political dissidents were often diagnosed as insane and kept in mental hospitals because they did not conform to party rules.

DEVIATION FROM IDEAL MENTAL HEALTH

ASSUMPTIONS
- It is different from the other definitions in that it looks at the positive rather than the negative (i.e. it defines mental health – psychological abnormality only occurs in its absence).
- Jahoda identified six criteria for mental health.
- The fewer of these criteria that an individual meets, the more likely he or she is to develop mental disorder.

Jahoda's six criteria for mental health

1 Positive attitudes to self: high self-esteem and a strong sense of identity.

2 Self-actualisation: reaching goals and developing to your utmost ability.

3 Resistance to stress: developing effective strategies to cope with stress.

4 Personal autonomy: reliance on inner strength and ability to make decisions independently.

5 Accurate perception of reality: getting the balance right between unwarranted over-optimism or over-pessimism and living in the 'real world'.

6 Adapting to the environment: being competent in all areas of life and being flexible.

LIMITATIONS OF THE DEVIATION FROM MENTAL HEALTH DEFINITION

The difficulty of self-actualising
- The six criteria are a set of ideal standards. Very few people are actually able to meet them all.
- This means that the majority of people are abnormal by this definition, which does not make much sense.

Possible benefits of stress
- There is some evidence to suggest that moderate stress can actually provide motivation to achieve.
- Personal growth and individual autonomy are Western values. In many other collectivist cultures, this would be seen as unhealthy and abnormal.

Cultural issues
- Jahoda's idea are based on Western ideals of self-fulfilment and individuality.
- Jahoda's ideas are subjective – even within her own Western culture, there are variations of effective living.
- e.g. Do people really have to be autonomous to be happy and fulfilled?

DEFINING PSYCHOLOGICAL ABNORMALITY (3)

FAILURE TO FUNCTION ADEQUATELY

ASSUMPTIONS
- People with psychological disorders often show an inability to cope with everyday activities.

- This is such a common aspect of psychological disorder that it is taken into account when making a diagnosis.

- Individuals only need professional intervention if their behaviour is dysfunctional, i.e. they are self-harming, unable to carry out normal activities (e.g. hold down a job, maintain relationships) or are being caused distress.

Global Assessment of Functioning Scale (GAF)
- This is often part of the diagnostic procedure.
- It measures psychological, social and occupational functioning over the previous year on a scale of 0–100.
- At the top of the scale (100) there is superior functioning over a wide range of activities. At the bottom of the scale (under 10) – there is a persistent danger of hurting self or others *or* persistent inability to maintain minimal personal hygiene *or* serious suicidal act.

LIMITATIONS ASSOCIATED WITH THE FAILURE TO FUNCTION ADEQUATELY DEFINITION

Not the whole picture

- This does not really define abnormality – it simply determines the extent of the dysfunction or the likelihood that someone needs professional help.
- Psychological abnormality cannot be defined by dysfunction alone.

- People who go on hunger strike for a political cause are self-harming, i.e. dysfunctional, but would not necessarily be seen as abnormal.

Exceptions to the rule

- People sometimes behave dysfunctionally temporarily in response to stress.

- Students might experience extreme anxiety before exams and neglect personal hygiene, normal sleep habits, etc. but this would not be seen as psychological abnormality.

- Some people behave dysfunctionally in terms of their aggressive/violent response to other people, but experience no personal distress or perceived inability to cope with life.

- Psychopaths show little personal distress or sense of inadequacy and yet their behaviour often goes beyond what is thought to be normal.

Cultural issues

- Inability to cope might be the cause of mental disorder rather than a defining characteristic. This could explain why statistics show a higher incidence of psychological problems amongst ethnic minorities.

- Definitions of adequate functioning are based on cultural values about how we should live our lives.

- Minority ethnic groups are often subjected to prejudice and exploitation – this could lead to problems with psychological well-being.

- People from lower socio-economic groups or ethnic minorities might be diagnosed with mental disorders because their lifestyles are different, and so to white, middle-class psychiatrists, they seem not to be coping.

For practice in answering AS Psychology questions, why not use *Collins Exam Practice AS Psychology*?

TYPICAL QUESTIONS...

AO1 QUESTIONS

1 Outline any **two** definitions of abnormality. (3 + 3 marks)

Questions can name any of the definitions on the specification. Need to revise them all.

2 Describe any **one** definition of abnormality. (6 marks)

Less detail required for a 3-mark answer than for a 6-mark answer. Rough guide – one mark per minute.

3 Outline the statistical infrequency definition of abnormality and give **one** limitation. (3 + 3 marks)

Could be any one of the four different definitions in this type of question. Must read it carefully. Only one limitation asked for – mustn't waste time giving more.

4 Give **two** limitations of the deviation from social norms definition of abnormality. (3 + 3 marks)

Only limitations asked for here. Must not waste time describing the definition. Must make sure the limitations are relevant to the definition in the question.

AO1 + AO2 QUESTIONS

5 Outline and evaluate **any two** definitions of abnormality. (18 marks)

Only get credit for describing two – mustn't waste time describing any more although other definitions can be used to evaluate. Must remember the AO1/AO2 split – only 6 marks for description and the other 12 for evaluation/commentary.

6 'It is extremely hard to define abnormality adequately. Any definition has its limitations.' Discuss definitions of abnormality and their limitations. (18 marks)

Need to use at least two definitions in this kind of question but not necessary to write about all four. Remember the depth/breadth trade-off – more detail required on two definitions than on four.

BIOLOGICAL MODEL OF ABNORMALITY

MUST KNOW...
- Assumptions made by the biological model of abnormality in relation to the causes of abnormality.

MUST TAKE CARE...

Not to confuse **models of abnormality** with definitions. A **model** is an explanation for the origins of mental disorders, i.e. **why** they occur.

A model is important because it influences:
- the kind of research that is carried out into abnormality
- the kind of treatments offered to people with mental disorders.

BIOLOGICAL (MEDICAL) MODEL

Use the additional information in the green panels in a 6-mark answer.

1 Part of the brain might be damaged, e.g. Alzheimer's disease caused by loss/malformation of cells in parts of the nervous system.

3 The availability of certain chemical messengers (neurotransmitters) is thought to be a factor in causing certain mental disorders, e.g. an excess of dopamine in people with schizophrenia and a decrease of serotonin in people with depression.

ASSUMPTIONS

- Biological psychologists explain human behaviour in terms of physiological (bodily) causes.
- Mental disorders are thought to be related to the physical structure and functioning of the brain.
- There are four possible factors that can cause malfunctioning of these systems:
  1 Brain damage.
  2 Infection.
  3 Biochemistry.
  4 Genes.
- It is often called the medical model because it is the most widely accepted model of abnormality and is adopted by doctors.
- Psychiatrists treat psychological abnormality like physical disease.
- They see people with psychological abnormality as 'patients' who are 'ill' and require 'treatment' to 'cure' them of 'disease'.
- They classify disorders, seek underlying causes, develop appropriate treatments and devise methods of prevention.
- They assume that the most appropriate treatments are physical, e.g. drugs, surgery, ECT.

2 Infection can cause deterioration of brain cells, e.g. syphilis can lead to bizarre, paranoid behaviour.

4 There is some evidence from research (twin, family and adoption studies) that certain disorders can be passed on genetically. The evidence is strongest for schizophrenia and bi-polar disorder.

- It is not necessary to know about treatment in detail, but useful to know that:
  – it is an assumption of the model that psychological disorders can be treated using biological interventions (AO1)
  – the treatments have been criticised for dealing with symptoms and not causes (AO2).

EVALUATION OF THE BIOLOGICAL (MEDICAL) MODEL OF ABNORMALITY

Key
mauve = strength of model
yellow = weakness of model

No blame

- Diagnosis of mental illness removes sense of blame/responsibility from the individual. Means that other people are more likely to be sympathetic.

- This encourages the individual to become a passive patient who hands over responsibility for their 'wellness' to doctors. This could hinder their recovery.

Stigma

- Individuals with a label of mental illness are often shunned/avoided.

- Labels can lead to self-fulfilling prophesy. →

- e.g. Someone is diagnosed as depressed, then everything he or she does is interpreted in terms of his or her depression – this is then taken as evidence for the correctness of the original diagnosis.

Research

- A huge amount of research has been stimulated.

- This has increased our understanding about psychological disorders.

- Much of the evidence is inconclusive and can be difficult to interpret. ▶

- e.g. In family studies, it is difficult to distinguish genetic from environmental effects and, in studies of schizophrenia, it is difficult to decide whether increased levels of dopamine are the cause or the consequence of the disorder.

Treatments

- This model gives rise to treatments which can be successful in helping individuals with mental disorders to keep symptoms controlled.

- Some of the treatments are invasive, and side-effects can be irreversible.

- Many of the treatments only affect the symptoms and do nothing to deal with the underlying cause.

Reductionism

- This model is reductionist, but mental disorders involve complex mental and emotional processes and it seems unlikely that they can be explained purely in terms of brain cell activity.

PSYCHOLOGICAL MODELS OF ABNORMALITY (I)

Psychodynamic theorists believe that abnormal behaviour results from unconscious forces. The best known psychodynamic theory is Freud's theory of psychoanalysis. It is fine to focus on that.

*The other three models on the specification are **psychological models**:*
- *psychodynamic*
- *behavioural*
- *cognitive.*

PSYCHODYNAMIC MODEL

Use the additional information in the green panels in a 6-mark answer.

ASSUMPTIONS

- Mental disorders arise from the dynamics of the psyche, i.e. they have psychological rather than physical causes.
- The psyche consists of three interrelated systems: the id, the ego and the superego.
- These systems are in constant conflict because they are fired by different motives.
- These conflicts are unconscious and we are unaware of them at a conscious level.
- Well-adjusted people have strong egos that can balance the demands of the id and the ego.
- The ego uses defence mechanisms like repression to help reduce the anxiety caused by conflict.
- Defence mechanisms can help in the short-term, but if over-used, can create psychological problems.
- If the ego is weakened, either the id or the superego can gain the upper hand – this will lead to personality disturbances, i.e. psychological problems.
- Psychical conflict can occur at any time but is most common in early childhood when the ego is immature.
- Children go through a series of psychosexual stages and conflict can arise at any one of these.
- Children use repression to push distressing events into the unconscious but the associated anxiety can come out in dreams and odd behaviour and may cause psychological disorders.
- Psychological disorders can only be resolved by uncovering the original unconscious conflict to gain insight.

Id: pleasure-orientated, wants instant gratification.

Ego: reality-based, tries to referee between the id and the superego.

Superego: conscience, sense of right and wrong.

Repression: pushing unacceptable memories into the unconscious.

Projection: blaming someone else.

Denial: refusal to admit to feeling certain emotions.

Displacement: venting feelings on someone other than the real target.

Regression: behaving like a child.

Failure to resolve conflicts at any of the stages can affect personality and cause later psychological disturbance:
- oral – conflict focuses on weaning
- anal – conflict focuses on toilet training
- phallic – conflict focuses on relationship with parents.

EVALUATION OF THE PSYCHODYNAMIC MODEL OF ABNORMALITY

Influence

- Freud's theory has been very influential and changed people's thinking about people who have mental disorders.
- First model to establish talking therapy as an acceptable form of treatment.

Key
mauve = strength of model
yellow = weakness of model

Validity

- The model is difficult to test scientifically – critics claim this means that the theory is not valid.
- Supporters (e.g. Kline, 1988) say that a theory does not have to be tested scientifically to be valid.

Defence mechanisms and childhood experience

- It is difficult to demonstrate defence mechanisms experimentally.
- There is some research that supports the idea that adults with psychological problems often experienced childhood trauma.
- Research into childhood trauma involves retrospective data that could be unreliable.

Relevance

- Some critics say the model is culture-bound and is not relevant today.

BEHAVIOURAL MODEL

Use the additional information in the green panels in a 6-mark answer.

Classical conditioning: repeated pairing of conditioned stimulus (CS), e.g. rat with unconditioned stimulus (UCS), e.g. sudden loud noise. This leads to conditioned response (CR) fear when the rat (CS) is presented alone.

Social learning: observational learning, i.e. copying models. Vicarious reinforcement is where behaviour is learned by seeing other people rewarded or punished for their behaviour.

ASSUMPTIONS
- This model focuses on behaviour, i.e. on what is observable.
- All behaviour, including abnormal behaviour, is learned through experience (i.e it is not an illness or a result of unconscious forces).
- Learning can occur through different processes:
  - classical conditioning
  - operant conditioning
  - social learning.
- The same basic laws governing behaviour apply to all animals. It is, therefore, acceptable to do research with rats, dogs, etc. and make generalisations to humans.
- What can be learned can be unlearned.

Operant conditioning: reinforcement (e.g. food) for spontaneously emitted behaviour, e.g. pressing a lever. Behaviour that is reinforced is likely to be repeated. Behaviour that is ignored is likely to extinguish.

PSYCHOLOGICAL MODELS OF ABNORMALITY (2)

EVALUATION OF THE BEHAVIOURAL MODEL OF ABNORMALITY

Focus on behaviour
- The behavioural model overcomes the ethical issue of labelling, by concentrating on the behaviour instead of the person.

Key
mauve = strength of model
yellow = weakness of model

Individual and cultural differences
- The model allows individual and cultural differences to be taken into account.

Underlying causes
- The model focuses only on the symptoms and ignores the causes of the abnormal behaviour.
- Behaviourists reject this criticism – they say the symptoms are the disorder.

Ethical issues
- Some people claim the therapies arising from the model are dehumanising and unethical.

Reductionism
- The model is simplistic and reductionist because it tries to explain abnormal behaviour in very narrow terms.
- It cannot explain all of abnormal behaviour (although it can explain some types, e.g. phobias, better than certain other models).

Research
- The simplicity of the model makes it easy to investigate the effects of learning on behaviour (e.g. 'Little Albert', Watson and Rayner's research (1920); Skinner's research).
- Much of the research on which the model is based was carried out on non-human animals.

COGNITIVE MODEL

> *Additional information to expand answer.*

- Ellis (1980) believed that irrational thinking shows in the language we use, e.g. 'I must get an A for my Psychology AS'; 'I ought to go running every day'; 'All the other students in my class should like me'.

ASSUMPTIONS

- Thinking and expectations guide our behaviour.
- When we think rationally, we behave rationally.
- We are usually in control of our own thoughts.
- Mental disorders arise from distortions in thinking, i.e. when there is faulty control of thinking.
- Everyone has disordered thoughts from time to time. Psychological problems only occur when the irrational thinking leads to maladaptive behaviour.
- If faulty thinking causes maladaptive behaviour, treatment should be effective if it encourages the individual to replace those thinking patterns with more positive, adaptive ones.

EVALUATION OF THE COGNITIVE MODEL OF ABNORMALITY

Key
mauve = strength of model
yellow = weakness of model

Model for living
- This model promotes psychological well-being and offers a way of coping with problems.

Research
- Research has shown that many people suffering from mental disorders do have thought patterns similar to those described by cognitive theorists.
- Most of the research is correlational – it might be that the negative thinking is a consequence of having a mental disorder rather than a cause.

Symptoms not causes
- The model does not explain why the irrational thinking occurs in the first place.
- The therapy aims at changing the thinking (i.e. the symptoms) and does not address the underlying causes.

Blame
- The individual is encouraged to take responsibility and to realise that he or she is in control.
- However, if the individual is held in sole responsibility, important, contributory situational factors might be ignored.

For practice in answering AS Psychology questions, why not use *Collins Exam Practice AS Psychology*?

TYPICAL QUESTIONS...

AO1 QUESTIONS

1 Describe the assumptions made by any **one** model of abnormality. (6 marks)

2 Outline **one** assumption of the biological model and **one** assumption of the behavioural model in relation to the causes of abnormality. (3 + 3 marks)

3 Outline the assumptions made by **one** psychological model and give **one** criticism of the model. (3 + 3 marks)

Any one psychological model is acceptable – must not write about the biological model.

AO2 QUESTION

4 Outline key features of the psychodynamic model of abnormality and consider strengths and weaknesses of this model. (18 marks)

CRITICAL ISSUE:
EATING DISORDERS (1)

DEFINITION

Eating disorders involve a serious disruption to healthy eating habits or appetite and can lead to abnormal psychological behaviour.

Anorexia nervosa: a type of eating disorder in which there is a compulsion to avoid eating food because of an unrealistic body image and an obsession about not becoming fat.

MUST REMEMBER...

Only **two** studies in detail required (APFCC):
- a study into **biological explanations** of eating disorders
- a study into **psychological explanations** of eating disorders.

Useful to know **some findings** from other relevant research.

Bulimia nervosa: a type of eating disorder in which there is a compulsion to binge. Bingeing is followed by self-induced vomiting or purging. There is a disturbance in self-perception of body weight or shape.

CLINICAL CHARACTERISTICS
OF ANOREXIA NERVOSA

Use the information in the mauve panels to expand answer.

- Refusal to maintain expected body weight. → Body weight is 85% or less of normal. Intense fear of gaining weight. Food intake restricted to approx. 600 calories per day. Avoidance of any food seen as fattening.

- Menstruation stops. → Early sign in females. Often precedes obvious weight loss.

- Ritualistic behaviour. → Food often cut up into tiny pieces. Odd eating rituals, e.g. chewing each mouthful twenty times.

- Preoccupation with food. → e.g. Reading cookery books and preparing food for other people.

- Distorted body perception. → Believe themselves to be overweight even when they are painfully thin.

- Mood disturbance. → Often show signs of depression, anxiety, mood swings and irritability.

- Denial. → Often deny the seriousness of their abnormally low weight.

- Physical effects of starvation. → Huge weight loss, dry skin, brittle nails, fine hair growth on body, thinning hair on scalp, reduced grey matter in brain. Effects of starvation can cause death.

CLINICAL CHARACTERISTICS OF BULIMIA NERVOSA

> Use the information in the mauve panels to expand answer.

- Binge-eating.
  - Recurrent episodes of uncontrollable binge-eating – triggered by stress.

- Compensatory behaviour.
  - Guilt and disgust lead to need to compensate for over-eating. Purging involves self-induced vomiting, misuse of laxatives, diuretics and enemas. Excessive exercise or fasting often follows binge episodes.

- Physical effects of bingeing and purging.
  - Increased risk of urinary infection and kidney disease; tendency to develop epileptic fits; repeated vomiting can damage tooth enamel.

- Body perception.
  - Distorted body image although body weight is usually within 10% of normal.

- Mood disturbance.
  - Depression is common. Bingeing may lead to feelings of suicide.

- Awareness.
  - Denial is rare in people with bulimia – they usually acknowledge they have a problem.

EXPLANATIONS OF EATING DISORDERS IN TERMS OF THE BIOLOGICAL MODEL OF ABNORMALITY

Most biological explanations relate to **genetic** or **biochemical/neuroanotomical** causes.

GENETIC EXPLANATION
Eating disorders are **inherited disorders**.

THEORIES/STUDIES	COMMENTARY
• Genetic science has not identified genes for specific behaviours associated with eating disorders, so research is based on twin and family studies.	• Not clear *what* is passed on genetically. Could be neurochemical abnormality, abnormal development of certain brain structures or the trait of obsessional behaviour.
• There is increased risk of eating disorders among first-degree relatives of people already diagnosed (APA, 1994).	• Relatives usually share same environment, so abnormal eating patterns could be learned.
• Holland et al. (1984) found greater concordance rates for anorexia nervosa in monozygotic (MZ) rather than dizygotic (DZ) twins – suggests there is some genetic basis.	• Small sample size; no concordance found in male twins; environmental factors not eliminated. Other research (e.g. Wade et al., 1998) into twins has found more evidence for environmental risk factors than genetic.
• Kendler et al. (1991) found evidence for genetic risk factors in bulimia nervosa, i.e. higher concordance in MZ twins than in DZ.	• They also found a significant number of environmental risk factors for bulimia, e.g. poor parental care, low self-esteem, history of dieting, fluctuating weight and date of birth. So, genes alone cannot be responsible.
• Hsu (1990) suggested that what is passed on genetically is a personality trait such as emotional instability. This makes the person more susceptible to stress, which in turn could lead to psychological disorders, including eating disorders.	• This idea is supported by research – in many cases, people with anorexia or bulimia have family histories of mood and personality disorders, but not necessarily eating disorders.

CRITICAL ISSUE: EATING DISORDERS (2)

BIOCHEMICAL/NEUROANATOMICAL EXPLANATIONS

Abnormal levels of neurochemicals (e.g. serotonin, adrenaline and cortisol) are responsible for eating disorders. Damage to the hypothalamus – a mechanism in the brain that controls the ANS and the endocrine system – can disrupt appetite and feelings of hunger and so could lead to eating disorders.

THEORIES/STUDIES	COMMENTARY
• Much of the research has focused on the hypothalamus. Animals stop eating – even starve themselves to death – when the hypothalamus is damaged.	• Research with humans can be difficult for ethical/practical reasons. Animal research is useful but has problems of generalisation.
• Keesey and Corbett (1983) have suggested that the hypothalamus works as a weight thermostat. A malfunction here could lead to eating disorders.	• A promising idea, but there is no conclusive evidence to show that this damage has occurred in all people with eating disorders.
• The hypothalamus also controls endocrine function. Research has found that endocrine levels in females with anorexia are depleted and similar to those of healthy nine-year old girls.	• Menstruation often stops before weight loss – suggests a disorder of the endocrine system. Again, there is no conclusive evidence to support this.
• Serotonin is known to have a role to play in appetite – increased serotonin activity is associated with suppressed appetite (i.e. it could be linked to anorexia) and decreased activity is associated with enhanced appetite (i.e. it could lead to bulimia).	• Anti-depressant drugs which increase serotonin levels are effective in decreasing binge-eating in people with bulimia.
• Jimerson et al. (1997) found significant differences between people with bulimia and controls in terms of serotonin function.	• It is difficult to disentangle cause and effect. Eating disorders have significant effects on the body and this might affect their biochemistry, i.e. starvation disrupts biochemical functioning and not the other way around.

*Only **one** study into biological explanations required in detail (APFCC).*

Aims
To investigate whether there is a genetic basis for anorexia nervosa using MZ and DZ twins.

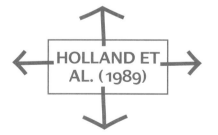

HOLLAND ET AL. (1989)

Findings
• High concordance rates found for MZ twins (55% to 7%). 5% of the co-twins did not have anorexia but had other psychiatric disorders.
• None of the male co-twins/triplets had anorexia.
• The male twin with anorexia in each pair was more disadvantaged at birth and the less dominant of the pair.

Procedures
• Participants = 30 pairs of female twins, 4 pairs of male twins and 1 set of male triplets.
• One of each pair had already been diagnosed with anorexia.
• Data were collected on the other twin/triplets to check for concordance.

Conclusions
• There is some genetic basis for anorexia, at least among females.
• No conclusions could be drawn about male twins because of low sample size.

Criticisms
• Higher concordance could be accounted for by shared environments.
• Sample size very small/unrepresentative so difficult to generalise.
• Even if there is a genetic component in anorexia, its contribution is small.

EXPLANATIONS OF EATING DISORDERS IN TERMS OF THE PSYCHOLOGICAL MODEL OF ABNORMALITY

Psychological explanations have been offered by all the major models: psychodynamic, behavioural and cognitive.

PSYCHODYNAMIC EXPLANATION

Eating is a substitute for sexual expression so eating disorders are a way of repressing sexual impulses.

THEORIES/STUDIES	COMMENTARY
• Bruch (1979) has expanded Freud's ideas. She suggested that anorexia is associated with psychosexual immaturity. For example, females who cannot face the responsibility of an adult role might starve themselves in order to remain childlike. In anxious mother/daughter relationships, this is mutually rewarding for both of them – the daughter can continue to depend on her mother and the mother can keep her 'baby'.	• As a result of starvation, menstruation stops and enlargement of breasts and hips does not occur (i.e. adult development is postponed). However, Bruch's conclusions were based on case studies – it is difficult to support her ideas experimentally.
• Eating disorders have been linked to traumatic experiences in early childhood, e.g. Wonderlich et al. (1996) found that women who had been sexually abused as children were more likely to develop bulimia than controls.	• This is correlational data and cannot demonstrate cause and effect. It is also based on retrospective data and might be unreliable. However, Wonderlich (2000) responded to this criticism by using data recorded when the girls were young and then later confirmed with them as adults.

BEHAVIOURAL EXPLANATION

Maladaptive eating patterns are learned through the processes of classical and operant conditioning and modelling.

THEORIES/STUDIES	COMMENTARY
• The individual learns to associate thinness with admiration and success/popularity. He or she starts to diet and gets admiration from friends/parents, etc. As the weight loss progresses, parents and friends become concerned and this attention is also rewarding. Starving can also be a way of punishing parents, which could be rewarding for a child of controlling parents.	• Operant conditioning techniques have been useful in helping some people with anorexia to gain weight – suggests that learning might play a part in the disorder. However, behavioural accounts do not address the reasons for the depression that often accompanies eating disorders.

• Cross-cultural studies have provided support for the behavioural idea. Eating disorders are more common in industrialised countries where food is plentiful but the ideal body shape is slim.
  – Immigrants into the USA, from cultures where eating disorders are rare, develop them just as frequently as those born in the USA once they have assimilated the ideals of attractiveness.
  – Nasser (1986) compared Egyptian girls studying either in London or in Cairo – 12% developed an eating disorder in London – but none in Cairo.
• Within Western cultures, there are some professions that place particular emphasis on slimness. Garner (1987) studied a group of female ballet students aged 11–14. 25% of them developed anorexia over a two-year follow-up period.
	• Few studies have been conducted in non-industrialised societies, so it is difficult to find a comparison.
	
	Mumford et al. (1991) found that girls from traditional Asian backgrounds living in Bradford were *more* likely to develop eating disorders than girls who had taken on more Western values.

• Social learning occurs through observation and imitation of models. The (predominantly female) body ideal depicted in magazines, on television, in films, etc. is thin.	• This explanation makes sense and can explain observed data such as gender difference (i.e. female stereotypes in the media are more associated with slimness than male stereotypes). However, in Western societies, we are all exposed to thin models but we do not all develop eating disorders.

CRITICAL ISSUE: EATING DISORDERS (3)

COGNITIVE EXPLANATION

Eating disorders are related to disordered thinking.

THEORIES/STUDIES	COMMENTARY
• People with eating disorders have distorted body images, i.e. they *think* they are unattractive because they *think* they are fat. They then *think* that they *must* diet in order to become more attractive.	• This kind of thinking is clearly inappropriate because people with eating disorders are often dangerously thin and are not attractive by normal standards.
• Bemis-Vitousek and Orimoto (1993) found that people with anorexia had the kind of thinking patterns predicted by the cognitive model of abnormality, e.g. 'I must lose weight as I am not yet thin'; 'I must lose weight so I can continue to be in control of my body'.	• This study shows good examples of maladaptive thinking – these girls were clearly not in control of their bodies because they were losing weight to a dangerous degree.
• Fairburn et al. (1999) compared people with eating disorders, people with other psychiatric disorders and controls. They found traits such as perfectionism and low self-esteem to be much more common in people with eating disorders.	• This fits with the cognitive model that predicts negative and/or unrealistic thinking. This model has suggested therapies designed to help people with eating disorders to think more realistically about themselves. A problem with this model is that it explains how eating disorders are maintained, but does not explain where the faulty thinking comes from in the first place.

MUST REMEMBER...

Only **one** study into **psychological explanations** of eating disorders is required (APFCC).

Aims
To investigate the role of self-esteem in eating disorders.

Procedures
• Measured self-esteem in 594 schoolgirls aged 11–12 years using validated self-esteem scale.
• 400 of the girls were followed up at age 15–16.
• They completed a questionnaire about eating and other psychological problems.

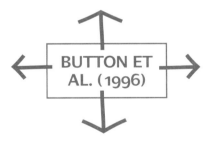

BUTTON ET AL. (1996)

Findings
• Low self-esteem at 11/12 correlated strongly with low self-esteem at 15/16.
• Girls with low self-esteem at 11/12 were significantly more likely to develop eating disorders than girls with higher self-esteem.
• Girls with low self-esteem at 11/12 were more likely to have other problems at 15/16 as well.

Conclusions
• Low self-esteem = significant risk factor for later eating disorders.
• Psychological factors seem to play a part in the development of eating disorders.
• Enhancing the self-esteem of children and young adolescents could be a strategy to help prevent eating disorders.

Criticisms
• Questionnaire data can be unreliable.
• The sample was biased – 60% came from social classes 1 and 2.
• Correlational data – does not show cause and effect.

OTHER PSYCHOLOGICAL EXPLANATIONS

Other psychological explanations not specifically rooted in the main models have focused on the role of family relationships in the origins of eating disorders.

INDIVIDUAL IDENTITY

- Parents exert a very strong level of **control** over child.
- At adolescence, child struggles against restrictions to **achieve own identity**.
- This can take the form of refusal to eat.

PRESSURE TO SUCCEED

- Anorexia is more common in middle-class families, where parents have **high-achieving**, professional backgrounds.
- Child feels there is too much **pressure** on them to achieve.
- Under pressure, child develops psychological problems, including anorexia.

FAMILY CONFLICT

- Based on Family Systems Theory (Minuchin et al., 1978).
- Conflict occurs in families, particularly between parents.
- Child develops anorexia in order to divert attention from the conflict.
- Child hopes this will focus the parents on a shared concern and bring them back together again.

Any of these could be used to expand an essay answer on the causes of eating disorders.

For practice in answering AS Psychology questions, why not use *Collins Exam Practice AS Psychology*?

TYPICAL QUESTIONS ...

AO1 QUESTIONS

1 Describe the clinical characteristics of any one eating disorder. (6 marks)

Must make it clear to the examiner which eating disorder is being described.

2 Outline the clinical characteristics of anorexia nervosa **and** of bulimia nervosa. (3 + 3 marks)

3 Describe the procedures and findings of any **one** study into the biological explanation of eating disorders. (6 marks)

Must read question carefully and choose an appropriate study – mustn't describe a study about psychological explanations if the question asks for one on biological explanations.

4 Describe the findings of **one** study into the psychological explanation of eating disorders and give **one** criticism of this study. (3 + 3 marks)

Must remember criticisms can be positive as well as negative.

This kind of question could ask for any combination of two from APFC.

AO2 QUESTIONS

5 Outline one explanation of eating disorders and evaluate this explanation using research studies and/or alternative explanations. (18 marks)

Make sure that you only outline one explanation (6 AO1 marks). Use the other explanations to evaluate – don't describe them!

RESEARCH STUDIES OF MAJORITY INFLUENCE

DEFINITION

Majority influence is a form of social influence where people adopt the behaviours, attitudes and values of other members of a reference group.

EXPANSION

• Some conformity to majority influence is based on the **desire to be liked** (normative influence), whilst at other times we conform because of our **desire to be right** (informational influence).

ASCH'S STUDY OF CONFORMITY (1956)

Aim

To see if participants would yield (conform) to majority influence and give incorrect answers in a situation where the correct answers were always obvious.

Procedures

• Seven male participants were shown a standard line and three comparison lines of different lengths.
• Participants had to say, in turn and out loud, which comparison line was the same length as the standard line (obvious).
• All participants, except the penultimate in each group, were accomplices of the experimenter.
• Accomplices gave unanimous wrong answers on 12 of the 18 trials. These were the critical trials.

Findings

• Participants conformed to the unanimous majority on 32% of the critical trials.
• 74% of participants conformed at least once and 26% never conformed.
• Some conforming participants claimed to have seen the same as the majority, others conformed because they didn't want to be ridiculed by the group.
• The majority who conformed did so because they thought their perception of the lines must be inaccurate and the majority's accurate.

Conclusions

• Even in unambiguous situations, there is still pressure to conform to a unanimous majority.
• Asch concluded that some people experience normative social influence and conform to avoid being rejected; others experience informational influence and conform because they doubt their own judgements.

Criticism

• The time and the place that the research was carried out might have affected the findings. In the 1950s, the USA was very conservative, and in the grip of McCarthyism, an anti-communist witchhunt, both of which placed greater pressure on people to conform and 'not rock the boat'.

SOCIAL INFLUENCE AND TYPES OF CONFORMITY

Normative social influence

▶ **public conformity**

compliance

Informational social influence

▶ **private conformity**

identification or internalisation (conversion)

OTHER RESEARCH FINDINGS ON MAJORITY INFLUENCE

Extensions to Asch's research

Asch found that levels of conformity dropped from 32% to 5% if one other participant dissented from the majority and agreed with the participant.

Perrin and Spencer (1980)
Replicated Asch's procedure using British students, and found only one conforming response in over 390 trials. They later used youths on probation as participants and probation officers as the majority. This time they found levels of conformity similar to Asch.

Smith and Bond (1998)
Reviewed 31 studies of conformity in different cultures. They found that people in collectivist cultures showed higher levels of conformity compared with those who lived in individualist cultures.

OTHER RESEARCH CONCLUSIONS ON MAJORITY INFLUENCE

Extensions to Asch's research

Asch concluded that a majority of three with no dissenters was more effective at producing conformity than a majority of eight with one other dissenter.

Perrin and Spencer (1980)
The researchers concluded that cultural changes over 30 years had led to a reduction in the tendency of students to conform. They also concluded that where the perceived costs of not conforming were high, conformity would be more likely.

Smith and Bond (1998)
They concluded that conformity was more evident in collectivist cultures than in individualist cultures because in collectivist cultures loyalty to the group is emphasised and in individualist cultures individual initiative is more highly valued.

These can be used as AO2 commentary but need to be built into an evaluative argument.

EVALUATION OF MAJORITY INFLUENCE RESEARCH

Conformity or independence?
Asch believed that his research actually showed how people could *resist* majority influence and remain independent. In 32% of the critical trials, participants conformed, which means that in 68% they remained independent, despite a unanimous majority.

Individual differences
Research has sometimes shown that women are more conforming than men, older people more set in their ways and less conforming to an experimental group than the young and that the less intelligent are more conforming than the smart. However, each of these has been found not to apply in some conformity situations.

Cultural effects
Perrin and Spencer argued that the Asch studies do not demonstrate a universal conformity effect, but a specific reaction to the cultural influences in the US in the 1950s (i.e. the era of McCarthyism).

Relevance of conformity research
Tanford and Penrod (1986) investigated whether decisions of jurors were influenced more by the weight of evidence in a trial, or by majority influence. They found that in nearly all cases, participants went along with the initial majority rather than being influenced by the evidence being presented.

TYPICAL QUESTIONS...

AO1 QUESTIONS

1 What is meant by the term 'majority influence' (conformity)? (2 marks)

2 Outline findings of research into majority influence. (6 marks)

3 Describe the aims and procedures of one study of majority influence. (6 marks) *Must be careful not to write anything about findings here.*

4 Describe the findings and conclusions of one study of majority influence. (6 marks)

5 Describe the conclusions and give one criticism of one study of majority influence. (6 marks) *This needs about 100 words of conclusions so may need to be creative!*

6 Give two criticisms of research into majority influence. (3 + 3 marks)

AO1 + AO2 QUESTION

7 Outline and evaluate research into majority influence. (18 marks)

RESEARCH STUDIES OF MINORITY INFLUENCE

DEFINITION
Minority influence is a form of social influence where a persuasive minority exerts pressure to change the attitudes or behaviours of the majority.

→

EXPANSION
• Minorities are most influential when they appear consistent and principled.

MOSCOVICI ET AL. (1969)

Aim

To see whether a consistent minority of participants could influence a majority to give an incorrect answer in a colour perception task.

Procedures

- 172 participants were used. All had good eyesight.
- Six participants at a time were asked to estimate the colour of 36 slides.
- All the slides were blue, but of differing levels of brightness.
- Two of the six participants were confederates of the experimenter.
- There were two conditions:
  – consistent (the two confederates called the slides green on all trials)
  – inconsistent (the two confederates called the slides green 24 times and blue 12 times).

Findings

- Participants in the consistent condition yielded and called the slides green in 8.4 of the trials.
- 32% of participants in the consistent condition reported a green slide at least once.
- Participants in the inconsistent condition yielded and called the slides green in only 1.3% of the trials.

OTHER RESEARCH FINDINGS ON MINORITY INFLUENCE

Moscovici and Nemeth (1974)
They found that seating position can affect minority influence. If a confederate (i.e. the minority) was *assigned* a seat, then seating position did not matter, but if they *chose* to sit at the head of the table, they had more influence.

Clark (1994)
Students read a summary of a murder case, and the jury's discussion. At various points in the 'trial' they were asked about the defendant's guilt. They were more likely to accept the minority position when they heard consistent persuasive arguments, and when they learned that more than one juror had 'defected' from the majority position.

Conclusions

- It is important for a minority to behave consistently over time if they are to influence a majority to change its viewpoint.
- Individual members of a minority must also be consistent, and there must be agreement among different members of the minority.
- Inconsistent minorities lack any real influence on majorities. Their opinions are viewed as groundless.

Criticism

- The artificiality of the laboratory setting in this experiment, and the relatively unimportant nature of the task, is unlike real-life situations where minorities such as pressure groups attempt to exert their influence on the majority opinion.

OTHER RESEARCH CONCLUSIONS ON MINORITY INFLUENCE

Moscovici and Nemeth (1974)
This study showed that, in terms of minority influence, *where* a person sits may be as important as what they say, or how confidently they say it.

Clark (1994)
Clark concluded that it was a combination of convincing arguments and a shift by other majority members that resulted in the minority exerting the greatest influence.

MUST REMEMBER...
To include conclusions from Moscovici et al. (1969) study if asked a question purely on 'conclusions' from minority influence research.

Majority influence tends to produce public compliance (conformity without acceptance) whereas minority influence tends to lead to conversion (private acceptance of minority position).

DIFFERENCES BETWEEN MAJORITY AND MINORITY INFLUENCE

Majority influence frequently involves the need for social approval (normative influence), whereas minority influence tends to involve the need for information about reality (informational influence).

EVALUATION OF MINORITY INFLUENCE RESEARCH
(from expert interview with Charlan Nemeth)

What lessons have we learned from minority influence research?
- Nemeth (2003) claims that people holding minority viewpoints are not just passive recipients of influence. They can actively **promote a differing viewpoint** which is sometimes accepted.
- We can also profit from minority views. Even when they are wrong, exposure to dissenting minority views **stimulates people to be better decision makers** and more creative in their thoughts.

Is minority influence more powerful than majority influence?
- Nemeth claims that the power of a minority is **not through direct influence**, but through indirect influence and the stimulation of thought. People will adopt the majority position either because they assume that the majority is right or because they don't want to face the rejection that going along with a minority viewpoint brings.

- However, the minority's **power comes from our reflection on the issue** after the confrontation. Because we think more broadly and more deeply after exposure to a minority position, their influence is potentially more powerful.

Do insights from minority influence research have applications in real life?
- One way is the law, especially **trial by jury**. The important issue is how do we best achieve the 'right' verdict? Because minority viewpoints stimulate better decision-making, they need to be protected.
- Research has shown that the **requirement of unanimity** in jury decisions (rather than some form of majority rule) increases the likelihood that minority views will be expressed and therefore increases the likelihood of justice.

TYPICAL QUESTIONS...

AO1 QUESTIONS

1 What is meant by the terms 'minority influence', 'majority influence' and 'social influence'? (2 + 2 + 2 marks)

2 (a) What is meant by the terms 'majority influence' and 'minority influence'? (2 + 2 marks)

(b) Give one difference between majority and minority influence. (2 marks)

Will need to ensure that the difference concerns the same characteristic (use 'whereas' in the middle).

3 Outline findings of research into minority influence. (6 marks)

4 Describe the aims and findings of one study of minority influence. (6 marks)

5 Describe the procedures and conclusions of one study of minority influence. (6 marks)

6 Describe the findings and give one criticism of one study of minority influence. (6 marks)

7 Give two criticisms of research into minority influence. (3 + 3 marks)

AO1 + AO2 QUESTION

8 Outline and evaluate research into minority influence. (18 marks)

*Take care not to confuse this with **majority** influence.*

EXPLANATIONS OF MAJORITY AND MINORITY INFLUENCE

MAJORITY INFLUENCE

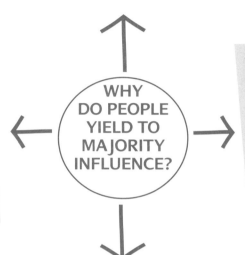

1 Cognitive dissonance
A participant is faced with two unpleasant choices in Asch's experiment. They can conform, in opposition to their true impressions, or they can dissent and face possible ridicule from the group. Both choices lead to cognitive dissonance, an unpleasant feeling that we have acted in the wrong way. A conforming participant could relieve their dissonance by blaming **group pressure** for their decision, leaving them with a clear conscience.

Only two of these would be required in an exam.

2 Normative social influence
Some people **go along with the majority** because of their **desire to be liked** by the rest of the group. We conform because we think others will approve and accept us because of this. Although we may go along with the majority in public (compliance), we may still hold to our own views in private.

WHY DO PEOPLE YIELD TO MAJORITY INFLUENCE?

3 Informational social influence
This type of influence is based on our **desire to be right**. **We look to others**, whom we believe to have more information than we have, to give us guidance about how to behave, particularly in novel or ambiguous situations. This type of influence can lead to internalisation, a long-lasting change of belief.

4 Natural selection
Conformity is necessary for the evolution of cooperation, i.e. for the selection of behaviours that are collectively useful. Over the course of evolution, those groups which have succeeded through cooperation tend to be the successful ones. Therefore the **urge to conform** and copy the behaviour of others is one which gives the group as a whole (and individuals within that group) an evolutionary advantage.

SUMMARY VERSIONS OF THE FOUR EXPLANATIONS

1 Cognitive dissonance
People may conform to overcome potential ridicule from group members, and then blame group pressure to overcome the resulting cognitive dissonance they experience.

2 Normative social influence
Some people go along with the majority because of their desire to be liked by the rest of the group.

3 Informational social influence
We conform because we believe others have more information than we have. We use others to guide us about how to behave.

4 Natural selection
Conformity is necessary for the evolution of cooperation; therefore the urge to conform is one which gives the group an evolutionary advantage.

MINORITY INFLUENCE

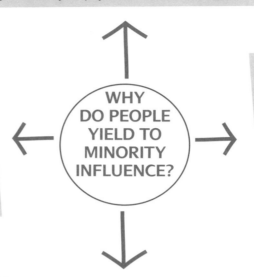

1 Consistency
The minority is only likely to have influence over the majority if they display **intra-individual consistency** (where a person maintains a consistent position over time), and **inter-individual consistency**, (where there is agreement among all members of the minority group). If the minority fails to display either of these, the majority is unlikely to pay them much attention.

2 The snowball effect
Once a few members of the majority start to move towards the minority position, then **the influence of the minority begins to gather momentum**, as more and more people gradually pay increasing attention to the potential correctness of the minority view.

WHY DO PEOPLE YIELD TO MINORITY INFLUENCE?

3 Group membership
We are most likely to be influenced by **those we perceive to be like us** (the in-group), and less likely to be influenced by those people we perceive to be not like us (the out-group). Minority influence is therefore more likely if we perceive a similarity between ourselves and the minority.

4 The dissociation model
A minority may influence majority group members through the process of **social cryptoamnesia** – the idea that ideas are absorbed into the majority viewpoint without them remembering where those ideas came from. Initially ideas are resisted because they arise from a minority position, but over time they become **detached from this source** and are later remembered without being associated with the minority.

SUMMARY VERSIONS OF THE FOUR EXPLANATIONS

1 Consistency
The minority is only likely to have influence over the majority if they display intra-individual consistency and inter-individual consistency.

2 The snowball effect
Once a few members of the majority start to move towards the minority position, then the influence of the minority begins to gather momentum.

3 Group membership
Minority influence is more likely if we perceive a similarity between ourselves and the minority.

4 The dissociation model
Over time ideas become detached from their source and are later remembered without being associated with the minority.

- - - - - - - - - - - - - - - -

TYPICAL QUESTIONS...

AO1 QUESTIONS

1   Outline two explanations of why people yield to majority influence. (3 + 3 marks)

Each explanation should be about 50 words. This is like saying 'Why do people conform?'

2   Outline two explanations of why people yield to minority influence. (3 + 3 marks)

*Need to give **explanations** rather than describe research into minority influence.*

RESEARCH STUDIES OF OBEDIENCE

DEFINITION

Obedience is an outcome of social influence where an individual acts according to a direct order from someone in authority.

→

EXPANSION

• It is assumed that without such an order, the person would not have acted in this way.

MILGRAM'S RESEARCH

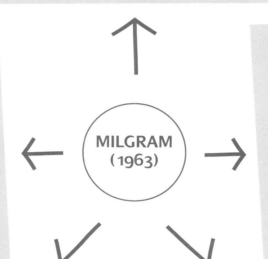

Aims
• One of the main aims was to explore the circumstances under which people might be induced to act against their conscience by inflicting harm on other people.
• Another aim was to explain the behaviour of those who committed atrocities in the Second World War death camps.

Procedures
• Milgram deceived 40 male volunteer participants into thinking they were giving gradually increasing electric shocks to another participant.
• The 'real' participant acted as the 'teacher' and the actor was the 'learner'. In this condition, the learner was in another room, with no voice contact.
• After each wrong answer an electric shock was delivered (although none were really given) with an increase of 15 volts each time up to 450 volts.

MILGRAM (1963)

Findings
• All 40 participants continued to at least the 300-volt level. 65% continued to the full 450 volts.
• The closer the 'teacher' was to the 'learner', the more likely they were to refuse the experimenter's command to deliver the shocks.
• Obedience levels were lower when the experimenter was not physically present and gave orders over the phone.

Conclusions
• Destructive obedience can be evoked in the majority of people by purely situational factors.
• When an individual is in a subordinate position within a powerful social hierarchy, they are liable to lose feelings of compassion and morality, and are inclined towards blind obedience.
• Milgram's research challenged the belief that behaviour such as the Nazi war crimes were a product of deviant personalities.

Criticism
• Orne and Holland (1968) claimed that Milgram's study lacked **internal validity** (participants did not really believe they were giving shocks and only pretended during the study) and **external validity** (it bore little resemblance to real-life situations such as Nazi war crimes).

DIFFERENCES BETWEEN CONFORMITY AND OBEDIENCE

◄ Public compliance and private change Obedience tends to involve no more than public compliance, with private attitudes left unchanged. Conformity can involve a long-lasting change if the individual internalises the views of the majority.

► Conscious versus unconscious effects Figures of authority often display signs of their authority (e.g. uniforms), and people are consciously aware they have obeyed an authority figure. However, people are often unaware they have been subjected to conformity pressures.

OTHER RESEARCH FINDINGS ON OBEDIENCE

Extensions to Milgram's research

Milgram found that obedience levels fell under the following conditions:

1 When participants were relocated to less prestigious surroundings.
2 When participants were forced to see, as well as hear, the pain and distress caused by their actions.
3 When the experimenter was not physically present and gave orders over the phone.
4 When there were rebellious peers, i.e. when others modelled disobedience for them.

Hofling et al. (1966)

In a study of obedience in a real-life setting, Hofling found that 21 out of 22 nurses agreed to administer a higher than maximum dose of a medication when instructed to do so over the telephone by a doctor. This was despite strict hospital rules prohibiting such actions.

OTHER RESEARCH CONCLUSIONS ON OBEDIENCE

Extensions to Milgram's research

These variations to the base-line study showed that:
1 An order is legitimised by the context in which it is given.
2 People are sometimes protected from the consequences of their obedience. Without these buffers, people will not obey so readily.
3 The authority figure exerts considerable social power over the individual, but this lessens if they are not physically present.
4 People tend to conform to the actions of others, particularly when they feel they are right.

Hofling et al. (1966)

This study showed that high levels of obedience can be obtained in real-life settings and so appears to provide support for the external validity of Milgram's findings.

> **MUST REMEMBER...**
> That conclusions can be used as part of the AO2 commentary.

EVALUATION OF OBEDIENCE RESEARCH

Validity of Milgram's study

- Orne and Holland (1968) claim that Milgram's study lacked both experimental and ecological validity.
- Milgram disputed these claims, arguing that participants showed considerable stress during the study and in post-experimental interviews said they believed they were giving shocks.
- Milgram's findings have been replicated in many other countries, supporting his claim that his study did have ecological validity.

Criticisms of Hofling's study

- Rank and Jacobson (1977) criticised the Hofling study, claiming that it did not represent most hospital situations.
- When they replicated the study using a known doctor, with a familiar drug (Valium) and with nurses allowed to consult another nurse before proceeding, only two out of 18 nurses obeyed the instruction.

The obedience alibi

- Mandel (2003) argues that the relevance of Milgram's findings as an explanation of events in the Holocaust is exaggerated.
- An exclusive focus on obedience detracts attention away from other explanations, such as racism and prejudice.
- The consequence of this is that it exonerates war criminals of their crimes by offering an 'obedience alibi' for their actions.

TYPICAL QUESTIONS...

AO1 QUESTIONS

1 Explain what is meant by 'obedience to authority'. (3 marks)

2 What is meant by the terms 'majority influence (conformity)' and 'obedience to authority', and give one difference between them. (2 + 2 + 2 marks)

3 Outline findings of research into obedience to authority. (6 marks)

This could just be the findings of Milgram's research or could include Hofling as well.

4 Outline conclusions of research into obedience to authority. (6 marks)

5 Describe the procedures and conclusions of one study of obedience to authority. (6 marks)

6 Describe the aims and conclusions of one study of obedience to authority. (6 marks)

7 Describe the findings and give one criticism of one study of obedience to authority. (6 marks)

AO1 + AO2 QUESTION

8 Outline and evaluate research into obedience to authority. (18 marks)

This could be the content of Q3 plus two paragraphs of AO2.

INTERNAL AND EXTERNAL VALIDITY IN OBEDIENCE RESEARCH

DEFINITION

Internal validity is a measure of whether experimental procedures actually work and whether the effects observed are caused by the experimental manipulation.

External validity is the degree to which the findings of study can be generalised beyond that specific situation.

EXPANSION

- Internal validity: e.g. participants may act according to what they think is expected of them (demand characteristics) rather than responding faithfully to the independent variable.
- External validity: this includes the degree to which the findings can be generalised to different people, different situations, and to different times.

INTERNAL VALIDITY AND OBEDIENCE RESEARCH

This material would be used as the AO1 content in a question on internal validity.

DID PARTICIPANTS IN MILGRAM'S STUDY REALLY BELIEVE THEY WERE GIVING SHOCKS OR DID THEY SEE THROUGH THE DECEPTION?

ORNE AND HOLLAND (1968)

Made three claims:

1 Participants search for clues about the real nature of an experiment, therefore their behaviour was a product of demand characteristics rather than obedience to authority.

2 Participants would have known the shocks weren't real because the experimenter didn't seem concerned, and could have given the shocks himself if necessary (therefore the participant himself was really the subject of the experiment).

3 Participants know that in Psychology experiments people don't really come to harm, so would have obeyed the experimenter safe in that knowledge.

INSIGHTS FROM RELATED RESEARCH

- Milgram questioned his participants one year after the study and found that 56% fully believed they had really been giving shocks (only 2.4% said they were sure the shocks weren't real).
- Holland (1967) replicated Milgram's study and found that when questioned afterwards, 75% of participants had not believed the deception.
- Rosenhan (1969) also replicated Milgram's study and found that 70% did believe they were giving shocks.

This material would be used as the AO2 content in a question on internal validity.

EVALUATION OF ORNE AND HOLLAND'S CLAIMS

1 Milgram defended his original conclusions through evidence from debriefing sessions. Participants admitted that they *had* believed they were giving shocks rather than using the 'excuse' that they had seen through the deception.

2 It is possible that those who refused to give shocks did not want to give up their 'hero' status, and so were reluctant to admit to having seen through the deception. This would have led to a false perception of whether participants accepted that what they were doing was real.

3 In some other obedience studies (e.g. Sheridan and King's study where shocks were given to puppies), the stress caused by giving electric shocks was more obvious, yet high levels of obedience were still found.

EXTERNAL VALIDITY AND OBEDIENCE RESEARCH

> *This material would be used as the AO1 content in a question on internal validity.*

DO THE FINDINGS FROM OBEDIENCE RESEARCH RELATE TO REAL-LIFE SETTINGS?

OBEDIENCE RESEARCH LACKS EXTERNAL VALIDITY

- Because Milgram's research took place in the artificial setting of a laboratory, it might be considered to be subject only to the rules that apply to that context, and have little relevance to behaviour in real-life settings.
- Orne and Holland (1968) claimed that the participants' behaviour reflected more their willingness to trust the experimenter and the experimental context than what they would do outside of the experimental situation.
- The instruction to give other people high levels of electric shock is essentially a ridiculous command, which would bear no relation to the type of instructions people would normally expect to receive from a legitimate authority figure in real-life.

INSIGHTS FROM RELATED RESEARCH

- Research in other cultures has supported the high levels of obedience found in Milgram's study, e.g. Mantell (1971) found 85% obedience in a German study, and Shanab and Yahya (1978) found 62% obedience in a study in Jordan.
- Meeus and Raaijmakers (1995) found that levels of obedience were even higher when participants were instructed to exert a more contemporary form of violence (being verbally hostile to a job applicant during an interview).
- Other research has suggested that humans may well have the capacity for destructive obedience, e.g. Latané and Darley (1970) found a low level of willingness to assist other individuals in emergencies.

> *This material would be used as the AO2 content in a question on external validity.*

EVALUATION

- There are important **differences** between Milgram's research and events in the real-world (e.g. the Holocaust):
  - Milgram's study took less than an hour per person, whereas those involved in the Holocaust were exposed to cruelty over many years;
  - in the Holocaust, people *knew* they were committing atrocities, whereas in Milgram's study they were reassured by the experimenter 'that there would be no permanent harm'.
- There are also **similarities**:
  - Milgram believed the same psychological process was involved in his study and in Holocaust events – the process of agentic shift;
  - in Milgram's study, obedient participants were more likely to blame the victim than were defiant participants. During the Holocaust, Nazi literature claimed Jews were personally responsible for their plight.
- Conclusions (Mandel, 2003):
  - the relevance of Milgram's findings to explaining the Holocaust has been greatly overstated;
  - the obedience explanation can be easily misused as an alibi to excuse those responsible for the Holocaust and other genocides.

> For practice in answering AS Psychology questions, why not use *Collins Exam Practice AS Psychology*?

TYPICAL QUESTIONS...

AO1 QUESTIONS

1 Explain what is meant by 'internal validity' and 'external validity'. (3 + 3 marks)

2 Explain the concept of internal validity with reference to one study of obedience. (6 marks)

Need to be explicit when relating this to a study. Don't just describe the study.

3 Explain the concept of external validity with reference to one study of obedience. (6 marks)

4 Consider the extent to which one or more studies of obedience might be said to have internal validity. (18 marks)

5 To what extent has research on obedience been shown to have external validity? (18 marks)

6 To what extent does research on obedience relate to the real world? (18 marks)

MUST REMEMBER...

That Q6 and Q7 are effectively the same question, and a question that doesn't specify **which** type of validity can be answered using either or both types.

EXPLANATIONS OF WHY PEOPLE OBEY AND HOW THEY MIGHT RESIST OBEDIENCE

WHY DO PEOPLE OBEY?

1 Legitimate authority
We have been socialised to **respect people with authority** and as a result we assume that they know what they are doing. **Legitimate social power** gives a person in authority the right to exert control over the behaviour of others, and others usually accept it.

2 Gradual commitment
Once people comply with a trivial, seemingly harmless, request, they find it **more difficult to refuse** to carry out more serious, escalating requests. In Milgram's study, because participants had to give greater and greater levels of shock, they found it difficult to refuse because each voltage increase was so small.

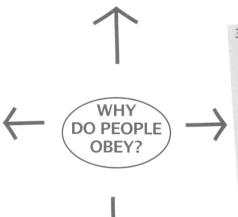

WHY DO PEOPLE OBEY?

3 Agency theory
Milgram believed that people operate either on the autonomous level, (they act voluntarily and are responsible for the consequences of their actions) or the **agentic level** (they see themselves as the **agents of others** and so **not responsible for their actions**). At the agentic level, people mindlessly accept the orders of the person seen as responsible for the situation.

Only two of these would be required in an exam.

4 Buffers
These are any aspect of a situation that **protects people from having to confront the consequences** of their actions. Milgram suggested that buffers (such as not being able to see or hear the victim) reduced the strain of carrying out an immoral command and so made it easier to obey.

SUMMARY VERSIONS OF THE FOUR EXPLANATIONS

1 Legitimate authority
Authority figures possess legitimate power which the person respects and therefore feels obliged to obey.

2 Gradual commitment
Having already complied with a trivial request, people find it more difficult to refuse to carry out more serious, escalating requests.

3 Agency theory
When people see themselves acting as the agents of others, they will mindlessly accept the orders of the person seen as responsible for the situation.

4 Buffers
Milgram suggested that buffers made it easier to obey because people did not have to confront the consequences of their actions.

HOW MIGHT PEOPLE RESIST OBEDIENCE?

1 Disobedient models
Exposing people to the actions of disobedient models **helps them to resist authority**. Although it is difficult to confront authority alone, the **presence of other rebels** may help a person see **resistance as legitimate**, and help them formulate personal strategies for disobedience.

2 Questioning motives
Questioning the **motives or legitimacy of authority figures** can help people resist obedience. Milgram found that when his study was transferred from the prestigious surroundings of Yale University to run-down offices, this made it easier for participants to question the legitimacy of the experimenter, and so obedience levels dropped.

HOW MIGHT PEOPLE RESIST OBEDIENCE?

3 Reactance
Blatant attempts to **illegitimately restrict a person's freedom** can sometimes produce a **'boomerang effect'**, causing them to do the opposite of what the authority figure is telling them to do. The more personally important the threatened behaviour, the greater the reactance. Reactance tends not be aroused by legitimate authority.

Other research hasn't supported Kohlberg's findings – could use this as an AO2 point in a part (c) question!

4 Individual differences
Kohlberg (1969) found that those who used **more advanced stages of moral reasoning** were better able to resist the commands of the experimenter in Milgram's study. Those who based their decisions on **higher moral principles** tended to be defiant when asked to deliver the higher levels of shock, whereas those at a lower level of moral development obeyed the experimenter completely.

SUMMARY VERSIONS OF THE FOUR EXPLANATIONS

1 Disobedient models
The presence of disobedient models may help the person to see resistance as legitimate, and help them formulate personal strategies for disobedience.

2 Questioning motives
Questioning the motives or legitimacy of authority figures can help people resist obedience.

3 Reactance
Attempts to illegitimately restrict a person's freedom can produce a 'boomerang effect', causing them to do the opposite of an authority figure's command.

4 Individual differences
Kohlberg found that those who used more advanced stages of moral reasoning were better able to resist the commands of the experimenter in Milgram's study.

TYPICAL QUESTIONS...

AO1 QUESTIONS

1 Outline two explanations of why people obey. (3 + 3 marks)

Each explanation should take about 2–3 minutes of writing time to maximise marks.

2 Outline two explanations of how people might resist obedience. (3 + 3 marks)

Could also use some of the insights from Milgram's research but must do more than just outline when participants resisted the authority figure.

ETHICAL ISSUES

DEFINITION

An ethical issue arises in research when there is a conflict between the rights and dignity of participants and the goals and outcomes of research.

Alternatively, could say it is when there is a conflict between the interests of the participant and the interests of the experimenter.

EXPANSION

- An example might be the right of the individual to give their informed consent, and the importance of studying behaviour in as natural a setting as possible.

DEFINITION/EXPLANATION

- Deception involves withholding information or misleading research participants.
- By deceiving research participants, we may remove their ability to give fully informed consent.

◀ DECEPTION ▼

EVALUATION

- In a survey where participants were asked, most people felt that minor deception was acceptable.
- Deception in studies of a trivial nature is less acceptable than in studies that make significant contributions to knowledge.
- Baumrind (1985) argued that deception is morally wrong on the basis of three generally accepted ethical rules: the right of informed consent, the obligation of researchers to protect the welfare of the participant and the responsibility of researchers to be trustworthy.

DEFINITION/EXPLANATION

- Participants should have sufficient information about a study to enable them to make an informed judgement about whether or not to take part.
- This may not be possible in all situations, as it may undermine the validity of the study.

◀ INFORMED CONSENT ▼

EVALUATION

- Epstein and Lasagna (1969) discovered that only one third of participants volunteering for an experiment really understood what was involved.
- Researcher should point out any likely risks of participation before fully informed consent can be given, but these are often difficult to predict. Milgram has claimed that he could not have foreseen the severity of the stress experienced by his participants.
- The issues of consent and withdrawal may be compromised by the payment of participants, who may then feel obliged to continue.

DEFINITION/EXPLANATION

- This means that research participants should be protected from undue risk during an investigation.
- These might include humiliation, embarrassment, loss of dignity or self-esteem.

◀ PROTECTION FROM PSYCHOLOGICAL HARM ▼

EVALUATION

- Zimbardo (see overleaf) admits that his prison simulation study was unethical because people suffered and the 'guards' were allowed to inflict pain and humiliation over an extended period of time.
- Baumrind (1964) claims that the distress caused during and after Milgram's experiment caused psychological damage to participants that cannot be justified.
- Aronson (2003) argues that human beings are not fragile, and can absorb an enormous amount of emotional discomfort without long-lasting negative effects.

ETHICAL ISSUES IN SOCIAL INFLUENCE RESEARCH

ETHICAL ISSUES IN MILGRAM'S STUDY OF OBEDIENCE

BAUMRIND'S CRITICISMS OF MILGRAM'S RESEARCH

- Baumrind (1964) claimed that Milgram placed his participants under great emotional strain.
- The distress caused to participants during and after the experiment caused psychological damage to them that could not be justified.
- It is unacceptable for innocent people to be put in these conditions just to enhance psychological knowledge.

MILGRAM'S RESPONSE (EVALUATION)

- The stress caused to participants was not anticipated prior to the study, and even in the most extreme cases participants were not permanently harmed.
- Participants were debriefed at the end of the study, including seeing that the 'victim' was unharmed.
- In a questionnaire completed by participants, 84% replied that they were glad to have taken part.

FURTHER EVALUATION

- Milgram's participants did not know the true purpose of the experiment, and therefore could not give their informed consent.
- Deception was necessary for the study to be realistic, but Orne and Holland (1968) claimed that it did not work.
- Brown (1986) argues that Milgram deserves praise for doing research of the highest human significance while showing great concern for the welfare of his participants.
- Mandel (2003) claims that obedience can be misused as an alibi to excuse those responsible for atrocities.

MUST TAKE CARE...
To consider the ethical issues in these studies, rather than just evaluate the studies in general terms.

ETHICAL ISSUES IN ZIMBARDO'S PRISON SIMULATION STUDY

ARONSON'S CRITICISMS OF ZIMBARDO ET AL.'S RESEARCH

Aronson (2003) claims that this study was unethical for the following reasons:

- The discomfort to participants was considerable.
- This discomfort went on for six full days.
- The investigators did not sufficiently protect the 'prisoners' from the excesses of the guards.
- Although the situation was dramatic, we didn't learn that much about prisons from the study.

ZIMBARDO'S RESPONSE (EVALUATION)

- The study was ethical, he claims, because it followed the guidelines of the Stanford University ethics committee.
- There was no deception, with all participants told in advance that if they were prisoners, many of their usual rights would be suspended during the study.
- However, Zimbardo admitted that it was also unethical, because people suffered and the 'guards' were allowed to inflict pain and humiliation over an extended period of time.

FURTHER EVALUATION

- Zimbardo admits that the study has not brought about the changes in prisons that he would have liked, therefore we might conclude that its *usefulness* was limited.
- Zimbardo claims that what was regarded as unacceptable about his and Milgram's research was not the methods, but the *findings*, which painted a darker side to human nature than people would like to admit.
- Zimbardo claims that as a result of research such as this, the pendulum has swung too far towards protecting research participants at the expense of new knowledge that could help society.

TYPICAL QUESTIONS...

AO1 QUESTIONS

1 Explain 'deception' and 'informed consent' in the context of psychological research. (3 + 3 marks)

2 Outline two ethical issues that have arisen in social influence research. (3 + 3 marks)

3 (a) Explain what is meant by 'protection of participants from psychological harm'. (3 marks)

(b) Illustrate your answer with reference to one study of social influence. (3 marks)

AO1+ AO2 QUESTION

5 Consider two or more ethical issues that have arisen in social influence research. (18 marks)

Don't confuse ethical issues with ethical guidelines.

DEALING WITH ETHICAL ISSUES

ETHICAL GUIDELINES

Each section (e.g. dealing with deception, dealing with consent, etc.) could count as a separate 'way'.

Informed consent
The investigators should inform the participants of **all aspects of the research** that might reasonably be expected to influence willingness to participate.

BPS = British Psychological Society
APA = American Psychological Association

Deception
The **withholding of information** or the **misleading of participants** is unacceptable if the participants are likely to show unease once debriefed.

ETHICAL GUIDELINES
- Ethical guidelines are a set of rules adopted by various institutions such as the BPS and the APA to guide the conduct of research.
- The role of the BPS guidelines is to 'preserve an overriding high regard for the well-being and dignity of research participants'.
- Consists of a series of statements clarifying appropriate conduct (e.g. deception, consent).
- Regular revisions of ethical guidelines reflect newly emergent issues in Psychology.
- They tend to be based on a 'cost-benefit' approach, i.e. scientific ends are seen as sometimes justifying the use of methods that sacrifice participants' welfare.

Protection from harm
Investigators have a responsibility **to protect participants from physical and mental harm** during the investigation. Normally the risk of harm must be no greater than in ordinary life.

Only guidelines
- Guidelines are **simply guidance** rather than hard-and-fast rules. They are also sometimes accused of being **vague and difficult to apply**.

CPA = Canadian Psychological Association

Limited scope
- Ethical guidelines may protect the immediate needs of research participants, but **may not deal with all the possible ways in which research may inflict harm** on people.
- The **CPA**, however, advises its members to analyse all likely long-term risks and benefits of each course of action on the individuals or groups involved or likely to be affected by the research.

EVALUATION OF ETHICAL GUIDELINES

Limited power of censure
- Most professional codes of conduct, particularly those in Psychology, have **very little power of censure** over their members.
- Exclusion from a professional body such as the BPS does not exclude psychologists from continuing to carry out research.

Research in sensitive areas
- The current BPS guidelines do not offer advice about what areas of research should or should not be carried out, or how the findings of research should be used.
- **They cannot, therefore, prevent researchers studying sensitive areas** such as racial differences in IQ, or prevent the misuse of findings that may arise in that research.

ETHICAL COMMITTEES

ETHICAL COMMITTEES

- Most research that involves human participants must first be approved by an ethics committee. Most organisations including universities have an ethics committee (or Institutional Review Board) that reviews all proposed research.

- An ethics committee is a group of individuals (typically researchers and administrators) whose role is to protect the rights of participants in research studies.

- Possible risks to research participants might be justified by anticipated benefits to the participants or to society as a whole. One of the major responsibilities of an ethics committee, therefore, is to assess the risks and benefits of proposed research.

- Because the welfare of the research participant is at stake, ethics committees must be able to discriminate between 'good' research and research that could potentially harm the participant.

MUST REMEMBER...

That ethical guidelines are one 'way' that psychologists deal with ethical issues; ethical committees are another, although their main role is to implement the appropriate ethical guidelines.

EVALUATION OF ETHICAL COMMITTEES

1 Malfeasance

Mueller and Furedy (2001) argue that researchers that would carry out the most unethical scientific studies are also the least likely to seek ethical approval for their research. The existence of ethical committees cannot, therefore, prevent unethical research.

2 No consensus on definition of risk

There may be a difference between the 'professional' and the 'public' perception of a problem, a claim supported by the fact that occasional incidents arise in research projects that reviewers have approved as ethically acceptable.

3 Lack of hard evidence

Mueller and Furedy claim that Psychology has yet to find any hard evidence that the existence of ethical committees has had any real effect in reducing ethical problems arising in psychological research.

For practice in answering AS Psychology questions, why not use *Collins Exam Practice AS Psychology*?

TYPICAL QUESTIONS...

AO1 QUESTIONS

1 Describe some of the ways that psychologists have attempted to deal with ethical issues in research. (6 marks)

*These could be **general** (e.g. the use of ethical guidelines) or **specific** (e.g. guidelines for specific ethical issues).*

2 Outline two ways in which psychologists have attempted to deal with ethical issues in research. (3 + 3 marks)

3 Outline one ethical issue that might arise in psychological research and outline one way in which psychologists might deal with this issue. (3 + 3 marks)

AO1 + AO2 QUESTION

4 Outline and evaluate ways in which psychologists have attempted to deal with the ethical issues that arise in psychological research. (18 marks)

Must be able to evaluate the use of ethical guidelines and ethical committees rather than just describe them.

QUANTITATIVE AND QUALITATIVE RESEARCH METHODS (I)

DEFINITION

Quantitative research: gathers information that can be analysed numerically.

Qualitative research: gathers information in a non-numerical, narrative form, e.g. pictures or speech.

QUANTITATIVE AND QUALITATIVE METHODS

1 Experiments (laboratory, field and natural).
2 Investigations using correlational analysis.
3 Naturalistic observations.
4 Questionnaires.
5 Interviews.

MUST KNOW...

- The nature and usage of various research methods and their advantages and weaknesses.
- The nature and usage of ethical guidelines.

MUST TAKE CARE...

To know the differences – they all look at the effect of the IV on the DV, but they vary in the amount of control possible (see page 94).

1 EXPERIMENTS

LABORATORY

Investigator manipulates the IV to see its effect on the DV in controlled conditions.

Advantages
- Replicable.
- Control of extraneous variables.
- Cause and effect can be established.

Weaknesses
- Artificiality leads to loss of validity.
- Can give rise to investigator and participant effects.

Ethical issues
- **Right to withdraw** – once in the formal setting, participants may feel that they must stay.
- Sometimes impossible to gain **informed consent** (leads to demand characteristic).
- **Deception** is sometimes used to avoid demand characteristics.

FIELD

Investigator manipulates the IV to see its effect on the DV in a natural environment, e.g. on the street or in the workplace.

Advantages
- Improved ecological validity.
- Reduction of demand characteristics.

Weaknesses
- Less control of extraneous variables than in a laboratory experiment.
- Difficult to replicate precisely.
- Little control over the sample of participants.

Ethical issues
- People often do not know they are participants and so **consent** – **deception** and **right to withdraw** are issues.
- **Confidentiality** – real-life organisations and people working in them must be protected with anonymity.

NATURAL

The investigator makes use of naturally occurring changes in the IV (i.e. does not have direct control of the IV).

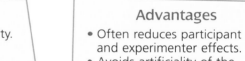

Advantages
- Often reduces participant and experimenter effects.
- Avoids artificiality of the laboratory.
- Allows investigation of events that could not be created in the laboratory or in field experiments.

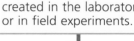

Weaknesses
- Lack of control of extraneous variables – reduces likelihood of cause and effect being established.
- Not possible to replicate or to generalise because the natural event is a one-off.

Ethical issues
- **Consent** and **right to withdraw** are issues.
- **Protection of participants from harm** – the natural event could be a disaster, e.g. a volcano eruption, and questioning of people involved might cause them further distress.
- **Confidentiality**.

2 INVESTIGATIONS USING CORRELATIONAL ANALYSIS

Nature and use	Correlational analysis is a technique for analysing data, which measures the strength of relationships between variables. The analysis will show if the relationship is **positive** (i.e. increase in one variable is associated with increase in the other variable), or **negative** (i.e. increase in one variable is associated with decrease in the other variable), or if there is no relationship at all.
Advantages	• Provides a precise, quantitative measure of the strength of relationships between variables. • Can be used to look at the relationships between many different variables at the same time – so is useful in unravelling complex relationships and for suggesting new hypotheses for further research. • Can be used to investigate issues where it is not possible to manipulate the variables.
Weaknesses	• Cannot establish cause and effect. • Cannot measure non-linear relationships (e.g. the U-shaped curve that shows the relationship between attention level and time of day).
Ethical issues	• **Consent** and **right to withdraw** – people are often not aware that data about them is being used for research. • **Use of findings** and ownership of data – correlational data must be handled sensitively as it is open to misinterpretation and can be used for reasons other than originally intended by the psychological researcher. Individuals should be guaranteed **confidentiality**.

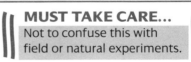

MUST TAKE CARE...
Not to confuse this with field or natural experiments.

3 NATURALISTIC OBSERVATIONS

Nature and use	Behaviour is observed and recorded in its natural setting and there is *no* deliberate manipulation of variables. No attempt is made by the investigator to influence the behaviour being observed. It is often used in studies of children or where the setting cannot be created in a laboratory, e.g. driver behaviour.
Advantages	• Has value as a preliminary research tool, i.e. can suggest hypotheses for further research. • Validity – can be a check on whether experimental findings can be generalised outside the laboratory. • Participants tend to behave naturally – either because they do not know they are being observed or because they have become used to the researcher.

Weaknesses	• Level of control over extraneous variables is poor and so it is difficult to be sure of cause and effect.
	• Observer effects:
	  – observer presence can inhibit participants being observed
	  – observers can be biased in their selection and interpretation of observed events.
	• Replicability – each observational setting is unique and so findings cannot easily be generalised.

Ethical issues	• **Privacy** – participants have a right to privacy. If they have not given consent, they can only be observed in public places where they could expect to be observed by other people. • **Confidentiality and consent** – researchers who observe people in places like hospital wards or school playgrounds should subsequently inform the people who have been observed and obtain consent to use the data. They should also guarantee anonymity. • **Use of findings** and ownership of data – data must be handled sensitively and not used for reasons other than originally intended by the psychological researcher.

QUANTITATIVE AND QUALITATIVE RESEARCH METHODS (2)

4 QUESTIONNAIRES

Closed questions: respondents have to choose either yes/no or from a fixed set of alternatives.

Open questions: respondents can use their own words and can express their views and opinions.

Nature and use	A questionnaire is a printed list of questions used to collect data from a large group of people. Questionnaire surveys can be conducted face-to-face, by post, by phone, via the internet or left in public places for participants to collect. Most surveys are carried out on carefully selected samples that are representative of the part of the population that is of interest to the researcher, e.g. single parents or A Level students.
	There are two main types of question: **closed** and **open**.
Advantages	• Quick, efficient and a relatively cheap way of collecting large amounts of data.
	• Data can be easily analysed (particularly form closed questions).
	• If the sample is representative, the findings can be generalised.
	• Surveys using questionnaires are usually easy to replicate.
Weaknesses	• The questions might be ambiguous, i.e. different people interpret them differently.
	• The questions (particularly closed ones) limit the type of responses.
	• Response rate is often below 50% – this can affect the representativeness of the sample.
	• Demand characteristics might operate and/or respondents might want to show themselves in a good light and so not be honest.
Ethical issues	• **Privacy** – respondents have the right to expect anonymity. If confidentiality cannot be guaranteed, the respondent should have right to withdraw data.
	• **Consent** – respondents need to know whether sensitive information will be asked for and how the data are going to be used before they agree to take part.
	• **Protection from harm** – if the questionnaire deals with sensitive topics, the respondents should be protected from stress, e.g. told that they do not have to fill in all the questions.
	• **Debriefing and support** – some questions might cause distress and there should be appropriate debriefing and support mechanisms made available.

5 INTERVIEWS

Unstructured interview:	Semi-structured interview:	Structured interview:
• Informal or in-depth conversation.	• A mixture of the two.	• Aims to produce quantitative data.
• Little is planned in advance (perhaps the first couple of questions).	• Some prepared questions.	• Questions are decided in advance.
• Allows interviewee to explain answers and introduce new issues.	• Some opportunities for interviewees to expand on answer.	• All participants are asked the same questions in the same order.
• Obtains rich, qualitative data.		• Answers not directly linked to the question are not followed up.
		• Very similar to questionnaire except questions are read out.

Nature and use	An interview involves the researcher asking the respondent questions. It may form the basis of a case study, it could be used as a way of conducting a survey or as a follow-up to other research methods (e.g. Milgram interviewed his participants after the initial study).
	Interviews can be **structured**, **semi-structured** or **unstructured**.
Advantages	Structured:
	• Focus is maintained on the topic under investigation.
	• Data analysis is simple and easier to generalise.
	• Less training required for interviewers.
	• Less risk of interviewer bias.
	• Interviewer on hand to clear up any ambiguities (unlike with most questionnaires).
	Unstructured:
	• Respondents can add information in order to explain their answers – this can open up important new insights and increases validity.
	• Researcher can follow up on issues raised by the interviewee.
	• Interview is more relaxed and informal so more trust can be built up – makes it more suitable for investigating sensitive topics.
Weaknesses	Structured:
	• Cannot follow up interesting answers.
	• Validity may be in question because of the formality of the situation.
	Unstructured:
	• Interviewer effects – the interviewer's own opinions/personal characteristics can affect the interviewee and the interviewer may interpret responses subjectively.
	• Demand characteristics such as social desirability bias can be a problem.
	• Interviewers need to be well trained and skilled – time-consuming and expensive.
	• Can be difficult to code and analyse the qualitative data obtained.
Ethical issues	• Respecting **privacy** and psychological well-being of interviewees.
	• Obtaining **informed consent** and respecting their **right to withdraw** data.
	• Maintaining **confidentiality** and anonymity.
	• **Protection from harm**.
	• Debriefing and support.

RESEARCH DESIGN AND IMPLEMENTATION (I)

AIMS AND HYPOTHESES

MUST KNOW...
- How to formulate aims and hypotheses.
- Factors involved in designing experiments and non-experimental investigations.

DEFINITION

Aim: the intended purpose of an investigation, i.e. what the investigation is trying to discover.

DEFINITION

Alternative/Experimental hypothesis: a prediction that something other than chance alone will produce certain results. It must be formulated as a testable statement. An alternative or experimental hypothesis can be directional or non-directional

DEFINITION

Null hypothesis: a prediction that there will be no differences between the results from the different conditions (or no correlation in an investigation using a correlation).

Directional: predicts the direction of the differences (or of the correlation in a correlational study). $\longrightarrow$

Non-directional: does not predict the direction of any differences (or any correlation in a correlational study). $\longleftrightarrow$

EXAMPLE
A researcher wants to investigate how items are coded in STM.

AIM
To investigate the nature of coding in STM and to see whether an acoustic or semantic code is preferred.

PROCEDURE
- The hypothesis must be testable so the investigator has to decide how to measure this. He or she decides to give participants two word lists: one set of acoustically similar words (e.g. cat, cap) and one set of semantically similar words (e.g. big, large). After each list has been read out, participants are immediately asked to write the words down in serial order.
- The researcher now has to make a choice between writing:
  – a directional hypothesis
  or
  – a non-directional hypothesis.

- He or she has read a lot of previous research and knows that people are likely to find the semantically similar words easier, i.e. she knows the direction the results are likely to go in (directional hypothesis). $\longrightarrow$
- Participants will recall more semantically similar words than acoustically similar words in an immediate serial recall test.

- Another researcher is not convinced by the previous research and wants to see for him/herself. He or she predicts that there will be a difference in recall but is not sure which way the difference will go. This researcher decides to use a non-directional hypothesis. $\longleftrightarrow$
- There will be a difference in the number of words recalled in a serial recall task depending on whether they are semantically similar or acoustically similar.

- Null-hypothesis: there will be no differences in the number of acoustically similar words and the number of semantically similar words. Any differences are due to chance.

EXPERIMENTAL DESIGN

Type of design	Advantages	Disadvantages
Repeated measures: same participants in each condition.	• Eliminates individual differences. • Fewer participants required.	• Order effects – participants may do better in the second condition through practice, or worse because of fatigue or boredom. • More likely to have demand characteristics. • Sometimes need to have a delay between conditions – time-consuming and can lead to loss of participants. • Sometimes need to generate two equivalent sets of stimulus material. • Cannot use it in some circumstances, e.g. comparing the effectiveness of two reading schemes – participants could not 'unlearn' what they had learned in the first condition.
Independent groups: different participants in each condition. Participants are randomly assigned to each condition to try to prevent bias.	• Eliminates order effects. • Less likely to have demand characteristics. • It can be less time-consuming. • No need to generate two equivalent sets of stimulus material. • It can be used where repeated measures design is impossible (e.g. because of order effects or if IV is something like gender).	• In spite of random allocation to the two conditions, there may be individual differences. • Twice as many participants are required than for a repeated measures design.
Matched participants: participants matched on relevant participant variables, e.g. gender, intelligence.	• Combines the advantages of both independent design and repeated measures design.	• Time-consuming and difficult to find matched pairs. • Difficult to decide on the relevant variables that need to be matched. • If matching involves some kind of pre-test, it could lead to demand characteristics.

NON-EXPERIMENTAL DESIGN

Naturalistic observations
- Sampling techniques – time interval, time point or event sampling?
- Identifying appropriate behavioural categories – is a pilot study needed?
- Recording data – tally charts, check lists or rating scales?
- Avoiding observer bias – use more than one observer but need to ensure observer reliability.
- Ethical issues – e.g. privacy, confidentiality, informed consent.

Questionnaires
- Type of data wanted – qualitative or quantitative, i.e. open or closed questions?
- Sampling – what is the target population? How to obtain a representative sample?
- Clear questions – avoid ambiguity, unnecessary jargon, double-barrelled questions, emotive questions and leading questions.
- Well-structured questionnaire – question order, use of distractor questions, avoiding response set, number of questions – might be useful to run pilot study.
- Ethical issues – e.g. confidentiality, right to withdraw.

DESIGN FACTORS TO CONSIDER

Interviews
- Preliminaries – identifying the research problem, linking to appropriate theory, deciding on the required categories of data, deciding on appropriate sample.
- Structure of interview – unstructured, semi-structured or structured?
- Questions – avoid ambiguity, social desirability, etc.
- Recording data – written notes, tape recorder? How to analyse qualitative data?
- Ethical issues – e.g. confidentiality, protection from harm.

RESEARCH DESIGN AND IMPLEMENTATION (2)

MUST KNOW...
- Factors associated with:
  - operationalisation of IV/DV
  - pilot studies
  - control of extraneous variables
  - ways of assessing and improving reliability and internal and external validity.
- Ethical issues associated with research design and ways of dealing with them.

THE OPERATIONALISATION OF THE IV/DV

MUST REMEMBER...

The **independent variable (IV)** is the variable manipulated by the investigator to see the effect on the DV.

The **dependent variable (DV)** is the variable measured by the investigator to see if it has been affected by the IV.

- **Operationalisation** means defining the variables so that the IV can be manipulated and the DV precisely measured. This makes the study replicable.

  EXAMPLE

  Age affects memory – how can we make this measurable (i.e. how can we operationalise the variables)?

  | Specify the age range. | Use a specific memory test. |

- People aged between 60 and 70 years will have shorter immediate digit spans than people aged between 20 and 30 years.
- The IV = the specific age range of the participants.

  The DV = the length of digit span (i.e. how many digits can be recalled in serial order from short-term memory).

CONDUCTING PILOT STUDIES

DEFINITION

A pilot study is a small-scale study carried out before the main investigation on a small sample.

EXPANSION

- It is used to find out if there are any problems with the design, the instructions for participants or the measuring instrument.
- Any errors can be corrected before the main study takes place, saving time and money.
- It also allows the researcher to practise any techniques needed for the main study and to see how long the study will take.

EXAMPLES

A pilot study before a questionnaire:
- to check that the instructions for filling it in are clear
- to check that the questions make sense, i.e. do not use jargon or complex language
- to check that the questions mean the same thing to different people.

A pilot study before a naturalistic observation:
- to help with the operationalisation of the variable, e.g. in a study on aggressive behaviour in the playground, it would be used to identify appropriate categories of behaviour
- to check reliability between observers.

CONTROL OF EXTRANEOUS VARIABLES

DEFINITION
Extraneous variables are any variables in the investigation other than the IV that might have an effect on the DV.

EXPANSION
- It is essential to control extraneous variables. If they are not controlled, we can't be sure the IV has brought about the change in the DV.
- Extraneous variables that are not controlled are called confounding variables because they confound (spoil) the results of the study.

MUST REMEMBER...
That it is difficult to eliminate all random errors. They are not as serious as constant errors since they are balanced out across conditions.

EXTRANEOUS VARIABLES CAN OPERATE IN TWO WAYS: RANDOMLY AND SYSTEMATICALLY

MUST REMEMBER...
That constant errors **must** be eliminated from the study otherwise the results will not be valid.

Random errors
These are extraneous variables which are unpredictable and unsystematic, i.e. they do not affect one condition more than the other.

Constant errors (systematic variation)
These are extraneous variables which vary from condition to condition, i.e. they affect one condition more than the other.

Examples
- A participant's state of mind, e.g. worried, happy.
- A participant's physical state, e.g. thirst, tired, hung over.
- A participant's level of motivation.
- Incidental noise, e.g. traffic noise outside.
- Room temperature.
- Previous experience on the day of the experiment, e.g. been in an argument, missed the bus.

Examples
- Failure to counterbalance presentation order of experimental conditions.
- Participant differences, e.g. elderly people in one condition and much younger ones in the other.
- Environmental factors that affect conditions differently, e.g. participants in one condition are tested in a very warm room while those in the other condition are tested in a cold room.

Choosing an appropriate design
e.g. Repeated measures design eliminates individual differences; independent measures design avoids order effects.

Standardisation of the environment (keeping variables constant)
e.g. Conditions in the laboratory kept the same for participants in both conditions (same level of light and heat, same time of day, etc.).

WAYS OF CONTROLLING EXTRANEOUS VARIABLES

Standardisation of the procedures
All the participants must be given the same set of instructions and the same amount of time to do the task and the same materials.

Randomisation
Can be used to decide the order of presentation of materials, e.g. participants are asked to rate 20 photos for attractiveness. If the photos are always presented in the same order, biases in rating might occur, so it is better to shuffle the photos each time to avoid bias.

Counterbalancing
Equal numbers of participants carry out the tasks in different orders as a way of avoiding order effects, e.g. in a repeated measures design comparing memory for words and pictures, one half of the participants do the word test first followed by the picture test and the other half do the pictures followed by the words.

RESEARCH DESIGN AND IMPLEMENTATION (3)

ASSESSING AND IMPROVING RELIABILITY AND INTERNAL AND EXTERNAL VALIDITY

DEFINITION

Reliability is concerned with the consistency of the results. If you carry out the study again using the same procedures and the same measures and get the same results, your study is reliable.

DEFINITION

Validity is concerned with the extent to which something measures what it says it's measuring.

DEFINITION

Internal validity is concerned with the extent to which we can be sure that the results are due to the independent variable (i.e. not due to extraneous variables).

DEFINITION

External validity is concerned with the extent to which research findings can be generalised:
• population validity – to other people
• ecological validity – to other settings.

ASSESSING AND IMPROVING RELIABILITY

Methods depend on the type of research method.

IN AN OBSERVATIONAL STUDY

Assessing
• All observers record data individually.
• Sets of data compared (correlated).
• High positive correlation = good observer reliability.

Improving
• Observers should be trained thoroughly.
• Operational definitions (e.g. what is an aggressive act?) should be clearly understood by all observers.

IN A TEST

Assessing
• **Split half method:** tests internal consistency of test items. Split the test items in two, score them and correlate the two sets of responses. Strong, positive correlation shows reliability.
• **Test–retest method:** tests reliability over time. Present the same participants with the same test on different occasions (with no feedback in between). Correlate the two scores – strong, positive correlation shows reliability.

Improving
• If correlation between the two sets of scores is weak, test items need to be revised.
• Check that the wording of question/test items is unambiguous and clear.
• Make sure instructions to participants are clear.

ASSESSING AND IMPROVING VALIDITY

Internal validity
• A study lacks **internal validity** if it is poorly designed and carried out, therefore to improve internal validity:
  – choose an appropriate design
  – control extraneous variables
  – reduce the likelihood of demand characteristics.

External validity
• A study lacks **external validity** if its findings cannot be generalised to other settings, therefore to improve external validity:
  – choose representative samples (i.e. include a range of ages, gender, class, ethnicity)
  – carry out investigations in realistic settings.

MUST REMEMBER...

That although laboratory studies are often low in ecological validity because of their artificiality, they are not **automatically** invalid. Similarly, field studies are not **automatically** ecologically valid.

ETHICAL ISSUES ASSOCIATED WITH RESEARCH DESIGN AND WAYS OF DEALING WITH THEM

MUST REMEMBER...
That ethical issues are also covered in Chapter 5 (Social Psychology), on pages 83–86.

Ethical guidelines for research with human participants have been published by the BPS (British Psychological Society) to help deal with ethical issues arising from psychological research. Ethical committees scrutinise research proposals to ensure participants' rights have been protected.

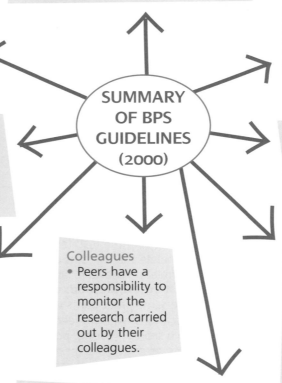

Consent
- Participants need enough information to make informed decision about whether to take part.
- In addition, parental consent required for children under 16.

Deception
- Should be avoided, but, if considered necessary, should be approved by peers or ethics committee.

Debriefing
- Participants should be debriefed and any deception explained.
- Researcher should make sure there are no misunderstandings or residual effects.

Right to withdraw
- Should be made plain to participants at outset even when payment has been given.
- Participants have right to withdraw retrospectively.

Confidentiality
- Participants have a right to expect this.
- If it cannot be guaranteed, they need to be warned so they can withdraw.

Protection
- Participants must be protected from emotional and physical harm.
- They must be reassured that they do not have to answer personal and private questions.
- Children – researchers must take care when discussing results with parents and teachers.

Colleagues
- Peers have a responsibility to monitor the research carried out by their colleagues.

Giving advice
- Researcher has obligation to inform participants if they feel there are physical or psychological problems of which the participant is not aware.
- Researcher should be able to refer to an expert source of advice.

Observational research
- Such studies must respect privacy and psychological well-being of participants.
- If participants are unaware of being observed, observation should only take place in public settings.

SUMMARY OF BPS GUIDELINES (2000)

RESEARCH DESIGN AND IMPLEMENTATION (4)

SAMPLING

DEFINITION

Target population: a group of people that share a given set of characteristics about which a researcher wants to draw conclusions, e.g. all students entered for AS Psychology in a particular year.

EXPANSION

- A target population is often too large to be investigated because:
  - it would take too long
  - it would cost too much
  - you might not have access to all members of the target population.
- Therefore, need to select a sample.

EXPANSION

- Researchers want to generalise from their findings. They can only do this if the sample is representative, i.e. the sample must share the characteristics of the larger target population. If the sample is *biased*, it does not represent the target population.

DEFINITION

Sample: a sub-set of the population, e.g. some of the students taking AS Psychology drawn from different schools and colleges across the country.

Example

Target population: all AS Psychology students.

Biased sample: a small number of students from one school or one town.

Representative sample: a large sample drawn from different types of school, different parts of the country and different ethnic and social backgrounds.

TYPES OF SAMPLING

	Random	Opportunity	Volunteer
Definition	Every person in the target population has an equal chance of being selected.	The researcher picks anyone who is available to take part.	A sample where participants self-select, i.e. they put themselves forward for inclusion.
How to obtain	• Put the names of all the members of the target population in a hat and pick out the required amount. • Obtain a list of all the people in the target population and give each name a number. Use a set of random numbers (e.g. computer-generated) to select the required amount.	• Ask people who are conveniently on hand, e.g. a class of students, a group of parents waiting to collect their children by the school gates, teachers in a school staff-room, etc.	• Advertise for volunteers, e.g. in a national newspaper, magazine or on a notice-board in a school, factory, etc. Sometimes offer money as an incentive. • Sometimes put questionnaires in magazines/newspapers and ask people to send in their answers.
Advantages	• Chances of selecting a biased sample are minimal.	• The most common technique because it is so convenient – participants are readily available so it saves time and money.	• Can be the only way of locating a particular category of participants, e.g. mothers with three or more children under the age of 5.
Disadvantages	• Does not guarantee that the sample will be representative of the whole population. • Can be difficult to get a list of the whole target population.	• Unlikely to be a representative sample, e.g. students are widely used who are not typical of the whole population. • Ethical issue – students might feel obliged to take part.	• Only a limited number of the target population will respond and they might not be typical of the population. This means the sample is likely to be unrepresentative.

THE RELATIONSHIP BETWEEN RESEARCHERS AND PARTICIPANTS

In any research study there is a temporary social relationship between the investigator and the participant. This means that the study could be affected by the interaction of those taking part, i.e. the participants and the investigators.

PARTICIPANTS

Might change their normal behaviour in some way because of the demands of the research situation, i.e. they might be affected by demand characteristics.

INVESTIGATORS

The researchers' own behaviour and particular characteristics might influence the outcome of the study, i.e. investigator effects.

EXPANSION

- Demand characteristics are the conscious or unconscious cues in an investigation that reveal the investigator's expectations, i.e. their hypothesis. Participants often react by trying to live up to these expectations or to present themselves in a favourable light.

EXPANSION

- Investigators are committed to their research and have invested time and effort. They naturally want their hypothesis to be supported and might influence the participants to bring this about. This desire to influence participants is usually unconscious.

Examples
- Trying to guess the aim of the research and then doing what they think the investigator expects (or sometimes, doing the opposite).
- Showing themselves in a good light, e.g. giving socially desirable responses in an interview/questionnaire rather than honest ones.

Examples
- Communicating to participants, in some way, what responses are expected, i.e. expectancy effect.
- Having personal characteristics, e.g. gender, age, social class, ethnicity, that affect the participants.
- Having mannerisms that affect the participants, e.g. smiling, nodding, frowning, tone of voice.

WAYS OF CONTROLLING PARTICIPANT AND INVESTIGATOR EFFECTS

Choosing an appropriate design
e.g. Demand characteristics are less likely in an independent measures design.

Choosing another research method
Many of the effects outlined above apply to laboratory experiments. In field experiments and naturalistic observations, participants are often unaware of being in a research study.

Deception
Can be used to avoid demand characteristics. However, this raises ethical issues.

Avoid contact with investigator
Instructions can be written down or presented on a computer screen.

Blind procedures
Do not entirely eliminate demand characteristics but can help to reduce them.

Single-blind
The participants understand the general aims of the research but do not know which condition they are in.

Double-blind
Research assistants are used to allocate participants to conditions, i.e. neither the investigator nor the participants know which condition they are in.

DATA ANALYSIS (I)

QUALITATIVE DATA

MUST KNOW...
- How to define qualitative data and to understand the strengths and weaknesses of using qualitative data.
- How to use and interpret medians, means, modes, ranges and standard deviations.

DEFINITION

Qualitative data come from observational research, questionnaires and interviews and are not in the form of numbers.

→

EXPANSION

- Observations often produce numerical data, e.g. the number of aggressive acts seen in the playground, but it can take the form of a tape-recorded conversation between a mother and child, a discussion in a classroom, diary descriptions, etc. This will provide qualitative data.
- Questionnaires using closed questions produce quantitative data but open questions produce qualitative data.
- Interviews usually give rise to qualitative data which can include:
  - what actually happened in the interview (e.g. what was said and what behaviour was observed)
  - interpretations made by the researcher
  - self-reports from the participants.

CONTENT ANALYSIS

DEFINITION

Content analysis is often used to analyse the content of books, TV programmes, etc., for example, to investigate gender stereotyping. It can also be used to analyse qualitative data from interviews and questionnaires.

EXPANSION

- Researcher collects (usually) large amounts of written notes and transcripts from audio and video recordings.
- By reading through, researcher begins to decide on coding units, i.e. categories for grouping similar items/themes together. Some items fall into more than one category.
- Researcher often uses a database system to set out the categories.
- Researcher produces reports based on the categories and on their own interpretations of the perspectives and feelings of the participants.
- Quotations from the participants are often included to show evidence for a particular interpretation.
- Researcher measures e.g. the number of times certain words or themes are mentioned and the amount of time that is given to them.

EVALUATION OF CONTENT ANALYSIS

Strengths	Weaknesses
- Produces **rich data** that can be used as the basis for further research. - Records not just what people say/do but **why** they say/do it. - Can be used to **assess what is omitted** from interview responses, texts, etc. and not just what is included. - Often has **high validity** because it is gathered in realistic/naturalistic settings.	- Interpretation of data can be **subjective** – researcher can be very selective in what he or she includes in the report. - Often **low in reliability** – although qualitative researchers try to use techniques to improve reliability, e.g. triangulation (= using more than one method of investigation to compare data).

MEASURES OF CENTRAL TENDENCY AND DISPERSION

MEASURES OF CENTRAL TENDENCY

DEFINITION

Measures of central tendency are single values that represent a set of numbers by giving the most typical value.

There are three of them:
• mode
• median
• mean.

They are used to summarise raw data to make it more understandable.

EXPANSION
• Mode: most frequently occurring value.
• Median: middle value when all the scores are put in order.
• Mean: the arithmetic average (i.e. add up all the scores and divide the total by the number of scores).

MUST REMEMBER...
That do not need to know about topics not included in the specification **but** useful to know what is meant by **levels of measurement** since these help to understand which measure of central tendency to use.

EVALUATION OF MEASURES OF CENTRAL TENDENCY

	Mode	Median	Mean
Advantages	• Easy to calculate. • Only measure that can be used for nominal data (i.e. categories of behaviour).	• Relatively unaffected by extreme scores. • Can be used on data with skewed distributions. • Can be used on ordinal and interval data.	• Makes use of all the available data. • The most powerful measure of central tendency.
Disadvantages	• Tells us nothing about the other scores in the set. • Often more than one mode in a set of scores so this limits its value.	• Does not work well with small data sets. • Can give a misleading impression if scores are clustered in high and low groups. • Can be affected by any alteration in the central values.	• Not suitable for use on data sets with extreme values. • Can only be used on interval or ratio data – not usually suitable for ordinal data.

MEASURES OF DISPERSION

DEFINITION

Measures of dispersion are measures that show the spread or variability of the scores. They show whether the scores in a data set are very similar to one another or whether they vary widely.

EXPANSION
• There are several measures of dispersion. The two on the specification are:
  – range: the difference between the highest and the lowest score in the data set
  – standard deviation: the variability of a set of scores from its mean – it measures the average amount each score deviates (differs) from the mean.

EVALUATION OF MEASURES OF DISPERSION

	Range	Standard deviation
Advantages	• Very quick and easy to calculate.	• Makes use of all the scores in the data set so is more precise than range. • The most powerful measure of dispersion.
Disadvantages	• It does not provide any idea of distribution around the central values because it only compares the lowest and highest scores. • It is seriously affected by extreme values in a data set.	• More complicated to calculate. • Can only be calculated on data measured on an interval or ratio scale.

DATA ANALYSIS (2)

See also page 91 for more on correlations.

MUST KNOW...
- What is meant by positive and negative correlations.
- How to interpret correlation coefficients.
- How to use and interpret histograms, bar charts and scattergraphs.

POSITIVE AND NEGATIVE CORRELATIONS

DEFINITION

Correlation refers to a statistical technique that measures the relationship between variables. A correlation exists when two or more variables co-vary. The relationship can be positive or negative.

Positive correlation: high values on one variable are associated with high values on the other variable, i.e. as values on one variable increase, so do values on the other variable.

Negative correlation: high values on one variable are associated with low values on the other variable, i.e. as values on one variable increase, values on the other variable decrease.

MUST REMEMBER...

Not to confuse a **negative correlation** with **no correlation**. A zero correlation exists when there is no relationship at all between the variables.

CORRELATION COEFFICIENTS

DEFINITION

A correlation coefficient is a statistic that measures the strength of the relationship between variables. The scale of measurement ranges from +1 (perfect positive correlation) to −1 (perfect negative correlation).

MUST REMEMBER...

That a correlation coefficient can only be measured by using a statistical test, e.g. Spearman's Rank Order test. It is not necessary to know how to do this for the AS exam.

INTERPRETING CORRELATION COEFFICIENTS

MUST REMEMBER...

That a correlation only shows the relationship between variables. It does not show cause and effect.

The strength of the correlation increases as the calculated value of the correlation coefficient moves away from zero and comes closer to either −1 or +1.

For example:

+ 0.79   shows a stronger positive correlation between variables than   + 0.65

and

− 0.87   shows a stronger negative correlation between variables than   − 0.72

One useful way to show the relationship between two sets of scores is to plot the values on a **scattergraph** (see page 103). This gives a visual guide as to the direction of the correlation. It is also useful in showing non-linear correlations.

GRAPHS AND CHARTS

BAR CHARTS

- Simple and effective way of presenting data.
- Usually used for nominal data (i.e. data placed in categories).
- Consist of a series of vertical bars of equal width.
- The categories are shown on the x-axis (horizontal axis).
- The frequency of each category (i.e. the number of times it was observed) is shown on the y-axis (vertical axis).
- Each bar represents a different category of data (discrete or non-continuous data), so the bars are drawn separately with a space between them.
- The bars can be drawn in any order (often placed alphabetically to avoid bias).

Example

Bar chart showing the number of observations of different behaviours in a group of children

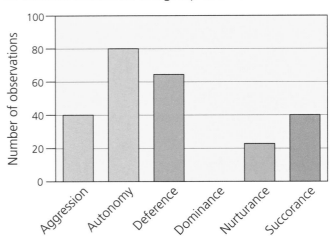

HISTOGRAMS

- One of the most widely used types of graph.
- Useful for presenting interval or ratio data.
- Consist of a series of vertical bars of equal width.
- The data are continuous so there are no spaces between the bars.
- The units of measurement/scores are set out on the x-axis.
- The height of each bar (i.e. as measured on the y-axis) represents the frequency of occurrence of each score/unit of measurement.
- Single values can be used on the x-axis, or, if the scale of measurement has a large number of points, the data can be grouped.

Examples

Histogram showing the number of words recalled in a memory experiement

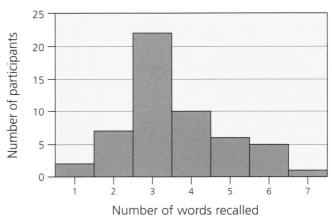

Histogram showing amount of time spent completing a spatial task

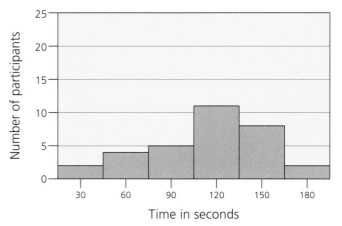

DATA ANALYSIS (3)

FREQUENCY POLYGON

- This can be used as an alternative to the histogram.
- It is useful for comparing two or more frequency distributions because they can be drawn on the same graph.

Example

Frequency polygon showing the number of words recalled in a memory experiment

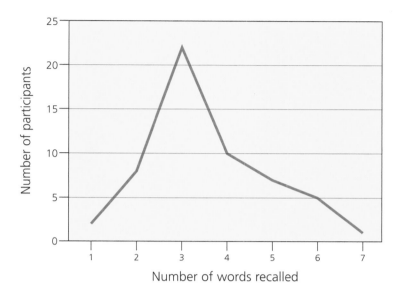

SCATTERGRAPH

- Useful for depicting correlational relationships.
- Data from one of the variables are presented on the x-axis and data from the other are presented on the y-axis.
- Each cross on the graph represents the scores on each of the two variables for one participant.

Example

Table showing the reading and spelling scores of a group of primary school children

Participant	Reading test score	Spelling test score
1	19	18
2	15	16
3	15	15
4	12	11
5	10	10
6	9	9
7	7	8

Scattergraph showing the same information

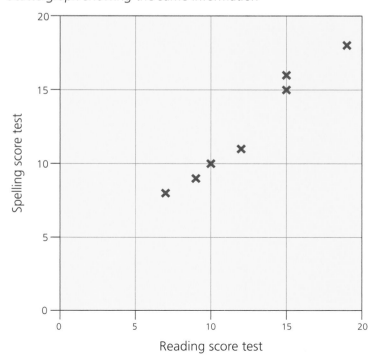

- A scattergraph is also useful to show non-linear correlations, i.e. relationships that seem to be positive at first, but then change to being negative, or vice versa.

Example

Relationship between time and day and attention level in students

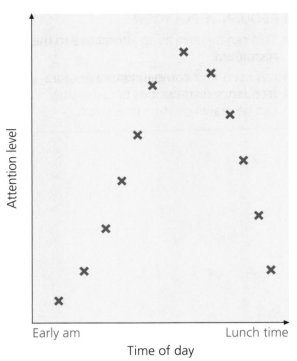

- The scattergraph will show whether there is a trend in favour of a positive or negative correlation. The closer the crosses lie on a straight line, the stronger the correlation.

Scattergraphs illustrating different correlation coefficients

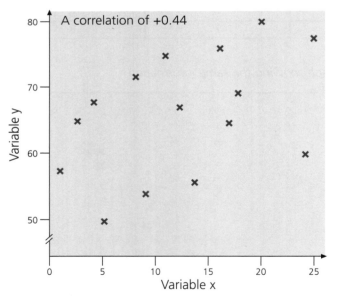

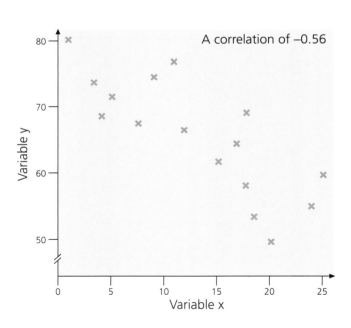

INDEX

ABOVE
AUSTRALIA

ABOVE
AUSTRALIA

A SALUTE TO HISTORY AND ACHIEVEMENT

PHOTOGRAPHED BY LEO MEIER

LANSDOWNE

Published by Lansdowne Publishing Pty Ltd
Level 1, 18 Argyle Street
Sydney NSW 2000, Australia

First published 1998

Photographs by Leo Meier

Publisher: Deborah Nixon
Production Manager: Sally Stokes
Project Co-ordinator/text: Joanne Holliman
Design: Anna Soo Design
Copy editor: Gill Hewitt

Set in Trajan, Bembo & Meta on QuarkXpress
Printed in Singapore by Kyodo Printing

National Library of Australia Cataloguing-in-Publication Data:

Above Australia: a salute to history and achievement
Includes index.
ISBN 1 86302 625 8.
1. Australia - Pictorial works.
919.4

FRONT COVER *The entrance to Coles Bay, Freycinet National Park, Tasmania.*
BACK COVER (TOP) *Sydney's magnificent Harbour Bridge;* (BOTTOM) *The night lights of Perth.*
ENDPAPERS *Tea plantations on the Atherton Tablelands in north Queensland.*
HALF TITLE PAGE *Beach huts on Brighton Beach, Melbourne.*
TITLE PAGE *Cape Leeuwin in south-west Western Australia.*
RIGHT *Constitution Dock at Hobart, Tasmania.*

CONTENTS

1 COASTLINES
Gateways to a Continent

2 CAPITAL CITIES
From Tents to Skyscrapers

3 WATERWAYS

The Search for an Inland Sea

4 RANGES AND FORESTS

Monumental Citadels

5 OUTBACK

Surviving All Odds

About the Australian Continent

Location: Southern Hemisphere

Latitudes: between 10° 41'S and 43° 39'S

Longitudes: between 113° 09'E and 153° 39'E

Extremities: from Cape York (north) to South-West Cape (south), 3138 kilometres; from Cape Byron (east) to Steep Point (west), 3983 kilometres

Total landmass: 7,782,300 square kilometres

Highest peak: Mount Kosciuszko 2228 metres

Surrounding oceans: Pacific (east), Southern (south), Indian (west)

Nearest neighbour: Papua New Guinea (200 kilometres north of Cape York)

Capital: Canberra

States/Territories: Australian Capital Territory, New South Wales, Victoria, Tasmania, South Australia, Western Australia, Northern Territory, Queensland

TORRES STRAIT

PACIFIC OCEAN

ARAFURA SEA

Thursday Island • Cape York

Melville Island

Jardine River NP

Bathurst Island

Darwin

South Alligator River

Kakadu NP

East Alligator River

ARNHEM LAND

Litchfield NP

Nitmiluk (Katherine Gorge) NP

Katherine River

Kununurra

River NP

RANGE

CAPE YORK PENINSULA

GULF OF CARPENTARIA

Lake Argyle

Gregory NP

BARKLY TABLELAND

Lakefield NP

Cooktown

CORAL SEA

Purnululu (Bungle Bungle) NP

Daintree NP

Trinity Bay
Green Island

Cairns

BUNGLE BUNGLE RANGE

NORTHERN TERRITORY

ATHERTON TABLELAND

Lawn Hill NP

Hinchinbrook Island

Townsville

GREAT

Tennant Creek •

Mount Isa •

Airlie Beach

Whitsunday Islands

BARRIER

e Mackay

• Devil's Marbles

DAVENPORT RANGE

QUEENSLAND

DIVIDING

REEF

DESERT

Finke Gorge NP

• **Alice Springs**

MACDONNELL RANGES

Diamantina NP

Rockhampton

Kings Canyon •

Carnarvon NP

RANGE

Uluru-Kata Tjuta NP

SIMPSON DESERT

Great Sandy NP

ETERMANN RANGES

Kulgera •

Simpson Desert NP

Fraser Island

Bundaberg

Tewantin-Noosa

Witjira NP

STURTS STONY DESERT

GLASSHOUSE MTNS

T VICTORIA DESERT

Goyder Lagoon

Brisbane

Lamington NP

Coober Pedy •

Lake Eyre

Lake Eyre NP

SOUTH AUSTRALIA

Byron Bay

Strzelecki Regional Reserve

Sturt NP

Glen Innes •

Dorrigo NP

Coffs Harbour

LARBOR PLAIN

Lake Torrens

Mootwingee NP

Lake Frome

Broken Hill

Darling River

NEW SOUTH WALES

Barrington Tops NP

FLINDERS RANGES

Wollemi NP

Newcastle

Lake Macquarie

Port Augusta

Mungo NP

EAT AUSTRALIA BIGHT

Blue Mtns NP

Sydney

Port Lincoln •

Adelaide

Murrumbidgee River

GREAT

Wollongong

Murray-Sunset NP

Murray River

Kosciuszko NP

Canberra

ACT

GULF ST VINCENT

Wyperfeld NP

Mt Buffalo NP

Lake Eucumbene

Flinders Chase NP

Kangaroo Island

Coorong NP

VICTORIA

Alpine NP

Ben Boyd NP

Croajingolong NP

Mount Gambier •

Grampians (Gariwerd) NP

Melbourne

Snowy River NP

Port Campbell NP

Twelve Apostles

Wilsons Promontory NP

TASMAN SEA

SOUTHERN OCEAN

BASS STRAIT

TASMANIA

Launceston

Freycinet NP

Franklin-Gordon Wild Rivers NP

Hobart

Cape Hauy
Cape Pillar
Cape Raoul

South West NP

N

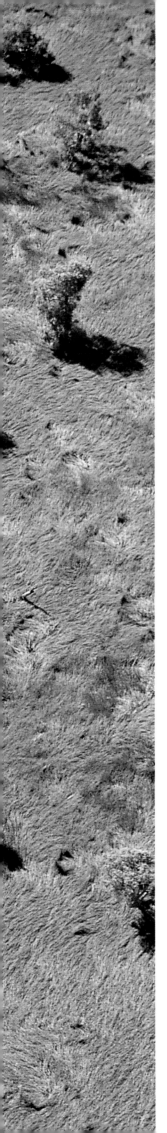

PREFACE

When I first arrived in this country I was astonished by its raw beauty and I consider myself incredibly lucky to have been able to capture on film over the past 25 years many of the diverse and contrasting images of Australia. In the early 1970s the population was much less than it is today and whenever I have the opportunity to look over my early photographs I find myself thinking about the march of time. I never tire of seeing the buildings of the central business districts grow taller and denser, rapidly changing the skylines; the city suburbs spread further to hug the contours of the coastlines; and the many areas of this country that will perhaps never be inhabited, leaving nature to run its own extraordinary course. Australia is a huge continent and it compares with nowhere else on earth. After all these years it still strikes a chord within me and by photographing it from the air I can offer others the opportunity of viewing the country through this unique perspective. It also means I can share with you the passion I have for this incredible country through those special shots that make all the hard work worthwhile.

Leo Meier

ABOVE *Australians love the beach and these dwellings in Perth follow the sweeping curve of the coastline.*

LEFT *After rain the colour of Kakadu's tall swirling grass is an outback surprise.*

FOLLOWING PAGES *The splendour of Sydney Harbour can be truly appreciated from above.*

INTRODUCTION

As you cross Australia by plane, it is easy to see distinct characteristics in the landscape. The way the vista changes, from coastal sand, surf and lushness, through lively city living, forests, ranges and undulating plains, to great tracts of deserts, is what makes the country so special. The land is the emotional heart of the nation and you need only witness the struggles between those who favour keeping the environment intact and those who want to reap the rewards of its vast resources to understand the strength of people's feelings towards this country.

ABOVE *This tall ship, docked at one of the old wharves in Sydney's Woolloomooloo Bay, is a replica of one of the earliest ships to arrive in Australia.*

A Salute to History and Achievement

When Europeans first arrived on these shores in January 1788, however, they lacked enthusiasm for their new home. For most it was a forced exile on the other side of the world, for others it was a duty to their government, for all it must have felt like banishment to a faraway place with alarmingly strange plants, animals and indigenous people. In the early years the settlers pitched their tents near a freshwater stream at a place they called Sydney Cove and struggled to eke out a living while waiting for extremely limited supplies to arrive from England.

The early explorers could venture only along the coastlines as blue-hazed box canyons to the west seemed impenetrable. It wasn't until 1813, when Gregory Blaxland, William Charles Wentworth and William Lawson charted a track across the Blue Mountains, that the pasture lands beyond became available to the fledgling colony.

LEFT *The Rocks district in Sydney was the site of the first British settlement in Australia. The area is now divided by the approach to the Harbour Bridge.*

These intrepid explorers, however, would not have found that pathway without the help of the Aboriginal guides who knew the land well.

It is estimated that Australia has been home to the Aborigines for more than 40,000 years, although according to their own Dreaming stories they have lived on the land forever. Each year, archaeologists seem to uncover new evidence which shifts the knowledge about this ancient culture's origins and lifestyles. What is now commonly accepted as true, despite the early misruling of *terra nullius*, is that by the time Europeans had arrived to colonise the country Aborigines had successfully occupied nearly all of the continent. Inevitably, there were clashes between the indigenes and the 'new Australians' and the complex debates about land ownership is still an emotional issue with no easy answers.

The two landmasses that make up the continent of Australia—the mainland and Tasmania—occupy a massive 7,682,300 square kilometres. This is more than thirty-two times the size of the United Kingdom, almost as large as the United States of America (excluding Alaska and Hawaii), and twenty times the size of Japan. As well as being large, Australia is also the flattest of the continent. The difference between its lowest point, Lake Eyre, and its highest peak, Mount Kosciuszko, is only 2243 metres, a quarter of the size of Mount Everest. It is perhaps easier to image the shape of the mainland as a large empty dinner plate—the coastal uplands being the rim, the central lowland the dip—whereas the plates of the other continents are piled high with

food waiting to be eaten. Australia as a continent has existed in its present form for a lot longer than the other landmasses and its surface has eroded over time. Additionally, there has been no volcanic activity for thousands of years to replenish its features.

When you consider the ratio of the country's population (nearly 18.5 million) to the vast surface area, most people would agree that 2.4 people for every square kilometre is more than generous, but a large portion of Australia cannot support permanent settlement. The continent's interior can be a harsh place, and unless you know where to look for water, food and shelter it can also be unforgiving.

The centre, referred to as the 'outback' by Australians, is mostly desert and rocky outcrops where little vegetation grows. Lake Eyre, a saltpan that extends 9300 square kilometres, is located in the inland region of South Australia. The most predominant image of the outback, however, is rolling red sand deserts, large rounded rocks, such as Uluru and Kata Tjuta, and hot, searing temperatures. It is all this, and much more.

Away from the centre the land very slowly rises into mountainous regions. Many scoff at the thought of these uplands being called 'mountainous' as Mount Kosciuszko is only 2228 metres above sea level and the average height of all the upland regions is as little as 300 metres above sea level. In the north

LEFT *Despite being the flattest of all the landmasses, the ranges in the south-east of the continent, where Mount Kosciuszko is located, are high enough to be covered in snow during winter.*

the highest points are along the Arnhem Land escarpment; in the west the Bungle Bungle and Hamersley ranges form part of the huge and ancient Western Plateau; in the south the Flinders Ranges rise north of Adelaide; and in the east is the Great Dividing Range, a series of broken plateaux with steep, east-facing escarpments. Mount Kosciuszko is located at the southern end of the Great Dividing Range in a section known as the Snowy Mountains.

East of the range, which runs from north to south down the continent, are the fertile coastal plains of Queensland, New South Wales and Victoria. Approximately seventy per cent of the population lives in this narrow band of land. The other major fertile regions of the country are in the south-west of the continent and in Tasmania.

All of Australia's capital cities, except for Canberra, were built near the coastline. This was because at the time of European colonisation the only transport to and from the country was by sea. As it turned out, these coastal regions would provide the most arable land with fresh water also more readily available in these areas than in other parts of the continent. Since those early days, the population has developed a thriving beach culture, which is not surprising considering that the country is surrounded by 36,735 kilometres of coastline.

Contemporary Australian culture has evolved from over sixty different nationalities and the reasons why people came to live in this country are many and varied. When the First Fleet arrived with 1487 passengers over two hundred years ago, it is estimated

there were between 200,000 and 750,000 Aboriginal people living on the continent. Today, there are a little over 300,000, about 1.7 per cent of the population.

During the gold rush era in the latter half of the 1800s, Chinese miners came to work the fields, but their arrival was met with hostility from the Europeans, who then imposed 'White Australia' laws that drove a large number home again. At around the same time, Pacific Islanders, indentured to work the sugarcane fields in north Queensland, also fell victim to government legislation and were forced to leave.

The twentieth century brought a worldwide movement of people that dramatically changed the largely British and Irish make-up of the population. After 1945, the government feared for the country's defence and increased immigration. Many people from war-torn Europe applied to enter the country and during the 1950s and 60s waves of migrants from the Mediterranean countries of Italy and Greece arrived. In more recent decades people have arrived from South America and Asia. Despite the shifts in ethnic origins, the majority of people granted the right to live and work in Australia today still come from the United Kingdom or New Zealand.

The history of any country is built upon everything that each person does as an individual and as a member of a community. Initially, Europeans tried to recreate their own homelands in this strange country. Many of the famous symbols of this nation, such as the Sydney Harbour Bridge and the Opera House, were achieved through great perseverance. Other icons, such as Uluru, existed long before humans trod the earth. To view these places from the air allows us to see the continent's contrasting and diverse features, from rugged and beautiful coastlines through lively city living to deserts that seem to roll on forever. The continent of Australia provides a myriad of images unique to this country only, and each in its own way salutes this incredible land.

OPPOSITE *On any given day the beaches around Australia attract crowds. Australians are known worldwide for their love of the sand and surf.*

LEFT *The way the sunlight falls upon the Australian landscape made it difficult for early painters to capture the country on canvas. Many tried to recreate European scenes, but the light in Australia is much brighter and most of the plants are unique.*

FOLLOWING PAGES *The moon, just rising on the horizon, is no match for the neon lights on Cairn's esplanade. Cairns is one of Australia premier coastal resort towns.*

COASTLINES

COASTLINES

The greatest concentration of the country's population is within the coastal plains. Such a high density on the rim of the country has occurred for a number of reasons: the cities were established in the seafaring era; the coastal plains provided easily accessible fresh water; and the east coast and the far south-west, where most people live, are the most fertile regions of a mainland considered barren and inhospitable. Before Europeans arrived, many Aboriginal groups used to congregate along the coastline for the same reason; it was where food sources were most abundant.

G a t e w a y s   t o   a   C o n t i n e n t

Australia, one of the world's largest islands, is a continent unto itself. The coastline, including the large island state of Tasmania in the south, is approximately 36,735 kilometres in length. Despite the country's deserved reputation for great surfing beaches, its coastline varies greatly in shape and form, from region to region. There are long, wide sandy beaches all around the country but in between these are weathered rocky outcrops that create dramatic seascapes. In the tropical north rainforests grow down hillsides to border the shoreline, while just offshore are simply stunning islands surrounded by reef. In coastal towns and capital cities everyone wants to live by the sea, so houses are built right next to the sand's edge.

TOP LEFT *Defying description, Cape Pillar is just one of Tasmania's striking coastline features.*

ABOVE *Bondi, Sydney's most famous beach, is only a seven-minute drive from the city centre.*

There are conflicting anthropological theories on the diaspora of the Aboriginal people. Some say they came to these shores from Asia over 40,000 years ago through a series of short island hops. Others propose the pathway went the other way, with their ancestors moving from this ancient continent to the northern climes, populating the world. Conclusive evidence may never be found to support either theory, but what is true is that the coastlines have provided access to and from Australia for many years.

Early cartographers hypothesised a landmass in the southern hemisphere to balance the northern continents. They called this land *Terra Australis Incognita* (Unknown Southern Land). Many sailors set forth to solve the mystery and after a number of near misses the first recorded sighting of Australia's coastline was in 1606 when Dutchman Willem Janszoon in the *Duyfken* charted the west coast of Cape York. Just a few months later Spanish seafarer Luis Vaez de Torres saw the tip of the Cape but thought it was just another island. Neither explorer realised the significance of their landfall.

The most important charting of the coastline in the seventeenth century was made by the Dutch navigator Abel Tasman, who mapped the south-west of Tasmania and the northern and western coasts of the mainland. There were many other sightings, landings and shipwrecks, particularly in the west, before that landmark day on 20 April 1770, when Lieutenant Zackary Hickes aboard the HM barque *Endeavour* yelled from the crow's nest, 'Land, ho!'. The ship's commander was Captain James Cook, and his epic journey brought vast changes to the continent.

ABOVE *The Captain Cook Highway winds its way along the picturesque coastline between the tropical tourist towns of Cairns and Port Douglas.*

Two great oceans wash the shores of the continent—the Pacific in the east and the Indian in the west—along with the Southern Ocean and the Arafura, Timor, Coral and Tasman seas. Between the mainland and Tasmania flows Bass Strait, and in the north between Cape York and the country's nearest neighbour, Papua New Guinea, lies Torres Strait. Approximately 1200 islands fall within the boundaries of Australia, including the overseas territories of Christmas, Cocos (Keeling), Heard and McDonald, Lord Howe, Macquarie and Norfolk islands.

Australia's islands range in size from Kangaroo Island, which is about 145 kilometres long and 55 kilometres wide, to the tiny coral cays within the Great Barrier Reef Marine Park. These latter islands, along with the continental islands of the Reef, provide some of the country's most picturesque coastal scenery. Many of these islands are deserted and protected as national parks while others, such as the Whitsundays, have resorts built on them.

The Great Barrier Reef runs south approximately 2000 kilometres from the mouth of the Fly River in New Guinea to Lady Elliot Island. This remarkable collection of coral clusters, the largest in the world, has created a vast tourist industry for Queensland. Coastal seaside towns, such as Cairns, have grown from service ports for local industries to thriving centres for holiday-makers. People's desire for access to the reef has created the difficult task of balancing construction and 'progress' with environmental concerns, so the Great Barrier Reef Marine Park was created by the Commonwealth Government in 1976 to protect the area's many natural wonders.

As the reef peters out in the south, the coastline becomes less protected from the surges of the ocean. Just off Bundaberg in Queensland lies Fraser Island, the world's largest sand island. Tall trees and even a rainforest grow upon the sandy base and crystal-clear lakes are perched within high dunes. The other large islands of the region are Moreton and North and South Stradbroke islands, lying just off the coast where the city of Brisbane stands. A short distance south is the popular tourist resort of the Gold Coast.

From this point down to Cape Howe in Victoria, the coastline shelves more steeply, providing deep, safe harbours such as Broken Bay, Pittwater and Port Jackson. All along the New South Wales coastline there are many coastal towns and inlets where people can enjoy the seaside holiday life.

As the land curves into Victoria, the underwater shelf continues down to Tasmania, where the steep headlands, wide sweeps of sandy beaches and secluded bays resemble the coastline of New South Wales.

ABOVE The high rolling hills on Kangaroo Island's north coast hide many secluded bays and inlets.

LEFT The Great Barrier Reef is so extensive that astronauts have seen it from outer space.

RIGHT Victoria's Port Campbell is sprayed by the Southern Ocean, which has for centuries pounded the coastline and created many interesting outcrops.

ABOVE *The limestone cliffs of Point D'Entrecasteaux are located along the spectacular south-west coastline.*

The difference between the two coastlines, though, is the lush green of Tasmania's flora, a result of lower temperatures and higher rainfall.

In Tasmania and along the south coast of the mainland the raging Southern Ocean has made savage indentations. The Twelve Apostles at Port Campbell no longer number twelve, four have collapsed into the sea with others threatening to follow. Further west from here the Great Australian Bight begins just beyond the Eyre Peninsula in South Australia. This huge inlet, like a great shark bite out of the base of the country, is bordered by a barren plateau called Bunda, after the Aboriginal name for the cliffs, while to the north is the expansive Nullarbor Plain.

The southern coastline of Western Australia features bold granite headlands and white sands. From the south-west corner to Perth are many popular beaches and national parks, while off-shore lies the Houtman Abrolhos—three groups of islands fringed by coral. These corals are the most southerly in the world and survive because warm waters sweep the region. Just to the north, on the mainland, are the Zuytdorp Cliffs, a notorious stretch where several early Dutch ships found a watery grave. These cliffs have been spectacularly carved from the Great Western Plateau, which is composed of some of the world's most ancient surface rock.

Shark Bay, near where Dutch sea captain Dirck Hartog landed in 1616, is a shallow inlet protected by the Peron Peninsula. Within its arms dolphins frolic with people in the waters at Monkey Mia, while at Hamelin Pool living stromatolites grow into large columnar shapes. These stromatolites are among the earliest organisms known in fossil records, and they exist in few other places in the world.

Along the north coast of Western Australia are the cliffs of the Kimberley region, which runs east towards the Northern Territory border. Melville Island, off Darwin in the Northern Territory, was the site of an attempt in 1824 to establish a colony in the north. It failed because there was insufficient fresh water and the Europeans settlers were unable to cope with the foreign landscape. After a number of other attempts, Darwin was finally selected as a settlement and the city has since been used extensively as a port of entry to and from Australia. During the Second World War the harbour played a strategic role in the allied naval operations in the Pacific and was subsequently bombed by the Japanese.

The western border of the Gulf of Carpentaria is Arnhem Land, an Aboriginal reserve covering 80,000 square kilometres. The terrain has made it difficult to build roads into this remote region and permission from the Aboriginal owners is required to enter the reserve. Offshore, in the north-east of the Gulf is Groote Eylandt, named by Abel Tasman. It is the largest island in the Gulf. The southern shoreline of the Gulf is characterised by tidal flood plains before curving up to the most northerly point of the mainland, the extensive Cape York.

In some of these northern areas it feels as if time has stood still. A large portion of Australia's coastlines have existed in their present form for many centuries, and while it is possible to imagine how ships foundered on the rough shorelines, it is more difficult to understand how some of the early sea explorers concluded that the country was uninhabitable. They obviously didn't realise the true extent of this island-continent's magnificent coastline.

ABOVE *Darwin's peaceful harbour has twice been shattered—by an air raid during the Second World War and by a cyclone on Christmas Day in 1974.*

LEFT *Cairns, once a quiet port serving only the rural industry, is now a true tropical paradise with large waterfront mansions, wide palm-lined roads, idyllic waterways and a bustling nightlife.*

TOP *Paragliding off the back of a boat is just one of the many daredevil rides on offer in the tropical north.*

ABOVE *Boats provide perfect transport around the coastline of Cairns. The calm water, provided by the extensive reef barrier, allows for safe passage.*

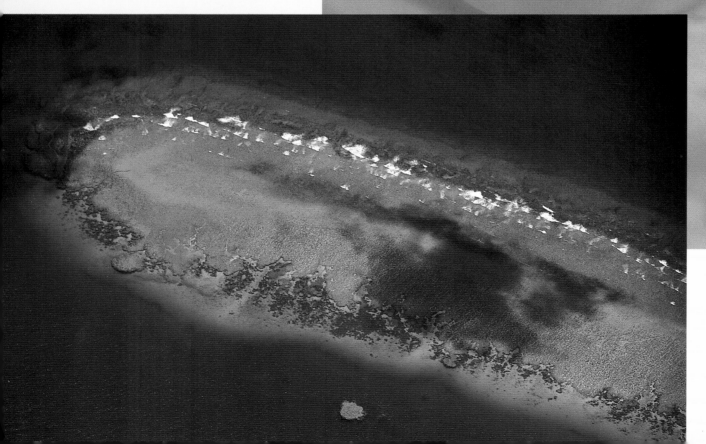

GREAT BARRIER REEF

The Great Barrier Reef Marine Park was founded in 1976 to protect 348,700 square kilometres of coastal waters comprising 3000 reefs, 969 islands, 400 species of coral, 4000 types of clams and snails, 1500 species of fish and a vast variety of crustaceans, turtles, whales, dolphins and birds. The Reef is a cluster of individual reefs aged between two and eighteen million years. They include island fringing reef (FAR LEFT) and the offshore Agincourt Reef (FAR LEFT BOTTOM). Some islands are continental (LEFT CENTRE), that is mountain tops from mainland cut off by rising sea water, while others, such as Green Island (LEFT & BELOW), are coral cays on which plants grow.

TOP *Fraser Island is the world's largest sand island and long white beaches sweep its 322 kilometres of coastline. A thriving rainforest has also managed to grow on the sand base.*

ABOVE *On the mainland south of Fraser Island is Double Island Point, so-named because of the way the water flows over a sand ridge creating an inlet.*

OPPOSITE *Redhead Beach on the New South Wales' coast is one of thousands of beaches between the Gold Coast and Sydney where resorts cater for holiday-makers.*

LEFT *South Head marks one side of the entrance to Sydney's deep harbour, Port Jackson. High rugged cliffs continue down the coast but give way to many beaches.*

BELOW *Looking north from Ben Buckler, the northern headland enclosing Bondi Beach, it is possible to see South Head, the entrance to Port Jackson and North Head.*

RIGHT *Sydney Harbour's North Head descends at Manly, but the small inlets of Shelly Beach and Fairy Bower are a prelude to the long, expansive Manly Beach, which is lined with stoic Norfolk pines.*

OPPOSITE *The famous Bondi Beach sweeps its way south towards other beachside suburbs, such as Tamarama, Bronte and Clovelly.*

ABOVE *Melbourne's Port Phillip Bay is a perfect spot for watersports, such as kayaking. The mouth of the Yarra River, which flows through the southern capital, is located at this expansive waterway.*

RIGHT *Within Port Phillip there are a number of boat launching points. The bay is enclosed by the two headlands, Mornington and Bellarine peninsulas.*

RIGHT *The mysterious-looking Twelve Apostles are sandstone outcrops cut adrift from the mainland by the Southern Ocean. They are near Port Campbell on the Great Ocean Road.*

OPPOSITE *Centuries of sea erosion has created many inlets along the Victorian coastline. The seaside cliffs are composed primarily of sandstone, which is fragile but has beautiful texture and colour.*

ABOVE The coastline of
Tasmania's wild South West
National Park is rugged and
isolated. Abel Tasman
charted this coastline in
1606 from the safety of his
ship, but to this day some
areas within the park have
never been explored.

RIGHT The east coast of
Tasmania is sometimes
called the Dolerite Coastline
because of the type of
basalt that fronts the ocean.
The incredible shapes of the
outcrops, such as these at
Cape Hauy on the western
side of the Tasman
Peninsula, are evidence of
the erosive might of the
coastal elements.

RIGHT *Cape Raoul, the eastern arm of the Tasman Peninsula, has eroded into long dark, spectacular columns that resemble organ pipes. About 165 million years ago molten dolerite forced its way between the sandstone base. When dolerite cools it contracts and breaks easily.*

BELOW *Sturdy red cliffs, which rise to peaks known as The Hazards, protect the beautiful Freycinet National Park from the raging sea. The park is a peninsula on the east coast of Tasmania.*

RIGHT *Maria Island is a national park, located six kilometres off Tasmania's east coast. It was once the site of a penal settlement and some of the buildings from that time still stand on the island.*

OPPOSITE *The city of Adelaide stretches to the eastern coastline of Gulf St Vincent. The beachside suburbs of Glenelg and Henley attract many holiday-makers.*

RIGHT *The newer Adelaide suburbs may look like doll's houses from the air, but they are perfectly poised so that everyone has a view of the waterway and their boat moorings.*

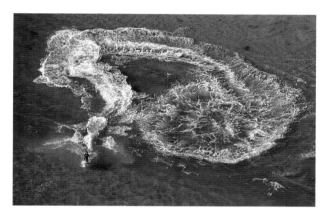

ABOVE *The Gulf is enclosed between two peninsulas: Yorke on the west and the Fleurieu on the east. This large inlet creates a wonderful location for watersports of all kind, including jetskiing.*

RIGHT *South of Adelaide on the Fleurieu Peninsula are a number of seaside towns that provide further access to the extensive gulf for fishing and pleasure craft.*

KANGAROO ISLAND

L ying off the South Australian coastline near Gulf St Vincent is Kangaroo Island, so-named by Matthew Flinders after he and his crew fed on the marsupials when they visited the island in 1802. Kangaroo Island is now a wildlife refuge. It is 145 kilometres long and 55 kilometres wide and is home to a number of national parks. The Flinders Chase National Park in the south-west corner contains the naturally-sculpted granite Remarkable Rocks (OPPOSITE TOP LEFT). They sit on the end of Kirkpatrick Point, a dome-shaped ledge which plunges 76 metres to the ocean. The steep western cliffs were the scene of a number of shipwrecks and around the island lighthouses are perched dramatically on cliff tops, such as the one at Cape St Albans (LEFT). The north coast, which faces towards the mainland, has a much quieter coastline with a number of peaceful inlets (OPPOSITE BOTTOM & OPPOSITE TOP RIGHT). The island's southern beaches (ABOVE), however, front the wild Southern Ocean and are often buffeted by Antarctic winds.

LEFT *Cape Leeuwin is located in the south-west of the continent, an area noted for its heath-covered granite head-lands and blue seas.*

RIGHT *Western Australia's Leeuwin–Naturaliste National Park stretches between the two capes of the same name. It is a beautiful area of rocky headlands and islets.*

ABOVE RIGHT *The country makes a defiant stop at the Great Australian Bight. These perpendicular, limestone cliffs, located between Point Culver and Twilight Cove, drop a startling 75 metres.*

RIGHT *Just north of Cape Naturaliste in Western Australia are long stretches of white sandy beaches. Not far from here is the noted wine producing region, Margaret River.*

OPPOSITE *Cottesloe in Perth is one of a long string of beaches that stretch north from the mouth of the Swan River.*

ABOVE & RIGHT *Perth residents are affectionately known as 'sandgropers'. These new suburbs being built right on the sea's doorstep may explain why. A number of waterside districts in Australia have created artificial waterways so that home owners can moor their boats nearby.*

LEFT *The warm seas that flow around the Houtman Abrolhos group of islands, offshore from Geraldton on the mid-Western Australian coastline, allow the world's most southerly reef to thrive.*

TOP *Bathurst Island, north of Darwin, is an Aboriginal reserve owned by the Tiwi Land Council. The island is separated from Melville Island by the very narrow Aspley Strait.*

ABOVE *This wet dock in Palmerston, a suburb of Darwin, is carved out of Clarence Strait. Palmerston was the original name of the Top End's capital.*

RIGHT *In Shoal Bay, east of Darwin, the mangrove-lined coastline was cleared so that a causeway could be built.*

CAPITAL CITIES

CAPITAL CITIES

From   Tents   to   Skyscrapers

The first image that comes to most people's minds when thinking of Australian cities is that of Sydney, particularly the scene comprising the harbour, the Opera House and the bridge. Port Jackson is, without doubt, one of the most beautiful settings for any city in the world. However, Sydney is just one of eight captial cities and all of these have grown into cosmopolitan metropolises from humble beginnings in a short period of time, and each has its own distinctive flavour, seasoned by its location and history.

Australia is divided into six states and two territories. These divisions began on 22 August 1770, when Captain James Cook took possession of the country's eastern seaboard in the name of King George III. He called this British acquisition New South Wales, but formal possession by the Crown was not effected until 7 February 1788, when the first governor, Captain Arthur Phillip, read his commission to the members of the First Fleet, who made up the residents of the new colony.

At that time, the western border of the colony was drawn along the 135th meridian of east longitude. While the map makers of the day were unaware of the whole shape of the continent, this line roughly divided the country into two, east and west, from a point near Darwin. Tasmania, known as

ABOVE *Once a licentious district, the area surrounding Campbells Cove on the eastern border of The Rocks has been transformed into five-star hotels, shops, restaurants and art galleries.*

PREVIOUS PAGES *The passengers of the First Fleet would not recognise their Sydney Town.*

RIGHT *Sydney's Harbour Bridge and Opera House are Australia's most famous features.*

Van Diemen's Land until 1855, was thought to be part of the mainland and hence part of New South Wales. In 1798, George Bass and Matthew Flinders circumnavigated the island, but it was not until 1825 that Tasmania became a separate colony. By that time the border of New South Wales had been moved further west to the 129th meridian.

In June 1829, a third colony, Western Australia, comprising the western seaboard of the mainland was proclaimed. In 1834, the province of South Australia was declared within the colony of New South Wales. This province became an independent colony when the first settlement was established two years later. The next colony to be founded was Victoria in 1851, followed by Queensland in 1859. At that time, the area north of South Australia was still known as New South Wales, but jurisdiction for the region was handed to South Australia in 1863 and it became known as the Northern Territory.

In 1901, the six colonies agreed to form a federation and they became known as states within the Commonwealth of Australia. Because of the rivalry between the capitals of New South Wales and Victoria it was decided that a new city would be built to house the nation's capital. In 1909, New

ABOVE RIGHT *The old and the new of Melbourne is captured by this modern glass office block and the Victorian architecture of Government House.*

RIGHT *The old warehouses at Salamanca Place in Hobart have been used as the model for the modern buildings behind them.*

ABOVE *The nation's impressive Parliament House was opened in 1988, the bicentenary year of Britain's colonisation of the country. Directly in front is the old parliament house, opened in 1927.*

South Wales surrendered land for the establishment of the Australian Capital Territory, where Canberra is now located. The final division of the states and territories took place in 1911 when the Northern Territory was transferred to commonwealth control.

Canberra is the federal capital of the nation but each state or territory also has its own governing or administrative body, which sits in their respective capital city. Apart from Canberra, each city started life as a penal colony or free settler town. It still seems extraordinary that within two hundred years these small communities have grown into thriving capitals where most of the residents enjoy a relatively high standard of living. There were many obstacles in the way of the early European inhabitants, not the least being their reluctance to accept the country's own unique environment, but the cities are now places of which the residents can be justly proud.

From austere and modest beginnings, Sydney now radiates around the spacious and awe-inspiring Port Jackson, which encompasses all the waterway from North and South heads to the mouth of the Parramatta River. The most famous images of this glittering city are the Harbour Bridge, majestically straddling the water between Milson's and Dawes points, and the Opera House, perched on the end of Bennelong Point. This city is the capital of New South Wales, often referred to as 'the First State' because it was from here that European colonisation of the Australian continent began after the War of Independence made it impossible for Britain to send its convicts to the American colonies.

SYDNEY

The First Fleet, under the command of Governor-in-Chief Captain Arthur Phillip, sailed 24,241 kilometres in 252 days to arrive at Port Jackson on 26 January 1788. Captain Phillip chose to establish his settlement at this site because Botany Bay, which was recommended by Captain James Cook, lacked sufficient fresh water. The Tank Stream supplied the colony with its water for a number of years until permanent reservoirs were built. The stream still flows into bustling Sydney Cove, home of Circular Quay, but it is now piped beneath tall buildings and busy city streets, and even, at one point, around an underground car park.

The city derived its name from the location of that first settlement, Sydney Cove, which honoured the then Home Secretary in the British Cabinet.

ABOVE *Farm Cove is picturesquely lined by the Botanic Gardens, Government House and the Opera House. The Harbour Bridge connects the city with the northern suburbs.*

BELOW *William Street, one of Sydney's busiest, funnels traffic to and from Kings Cross and Hyde Park on the city's eastern border.*

OPPOSITE *Sydney Tower, the city's tallest structure, has been a landmark since 1981.*

The passengers of the First Fleet consisted of 736 convicts (548 men and 188 women) and 17 children of convicts; 257 mariners, wives and children; and 20 officials—a total of 1030 people. The population of the city today is nearly four million and comprises an ancestral mix from over sixty different countries.

Sydney is relatively free of the violence and racial tensions seen in other major twentieth-century cities. This is perhaps because its people tend to have an egalitarian attitude towards life and enjoy a lifestyle that is relatively open and easygoing. On any given day, winter or summer, yachts will be out on the water; people will be picnicking by the harbour or wandering the foreshores, much of which has been retained as public parks; and commuters will be catching ferries to the city, or perhaps a train or bus across the bridge. Of course, Sydney is much more than a harbour hub— there are suburbs that spread all the way to the Blue Mountains; a run of beaches and rocky headlands that form the city's eastern border; tall skyscrapers; and a lively mixture of residents who enjoy everything this modern, sunny city has to offer.

OPPOSITE *The Opera House roof is composed of 1,056,000 tiles. The Opera House was opened in 1973, and on the hill behind is Government House, built in 1838.*

RIGHT *The Royal Botanic Gardens covers thirty hectares of land and joins the Domain to create a green belt along the city's eastern border. Many old buildings fringe these two parks: The Art Gallery (1909), St Mary's Cathedral (1868), those along Macquarie Street, Mitchell Library (1826), and The Conservatorium of Music (1821), once the stables of Government House.*

LEFT *The Cahill Expressway thunders over Circular Quay, a train station and the hub of harbour ferry transport. The Quay is located at Sydney Cove, which is also home to the Overseas Passenger Terminal.*

SYDNEY
HARBOUR
BRIDGE

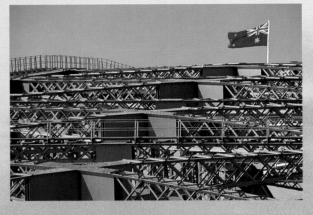

On 14 August 1930, under the watchful eye of a large portion of Sydney's population, the final central cantilever of the Sydney Harbour Bridge was put in place. It took nearly a century of debate and eleven years of construction before the vision of many, but the design of engineer J.J.C. Bradfield, was realised. The main span stretches 503 metres, the entire length of the bridge and its approaches are 1149 metres. The arch is made of silicon steel and its crown is 134 metres above sea level. The deck is made of carbon steel and its width is 49 metres, allowing for eight lanes of car traffic, two train tracks and a bicycle lane on the western side and a foot passage walkway on the eastern side. The total weight of the bridge is estimated to be 65,000 tonnes. The arch rests on four granite steel pins, which are covered by two 87-metre high granite pylons. The bridge was officially opened on 19 March 1932 by Premier Jack Lang, but in true Aussie larrikin-style the honour actually went to Francis Edward de Groot who, dressed in the right-wing New Guard uniform, thundered past the Premier and slashed the ribbon with his sword.

RIGHT *The Pyrmont side of Darling Harbour has been transformed from old workers' cottages to a large modern conference complex, shops, restaurants, hotels, city apartments, museums and entertainment venues.*

LEFT *Darling Harbour's waterfront esplanade is often the scene of impromptu and staged events and water taxis and other boats can berth right at the steps of this festive area.*

RIGHT *The architecturally stunning Glebe Island Bridge has become another landmark on the Sydney horizon. It spans Blackwattle Bay, linking the city with the western suburbs.*

OPPOSITE *The official residences of Admiralty House and Kirribilli House on the end of Kirribilli Point have the best views of the harbour. They are located on the north shore opposite the Opera House and near the tower blocks of North Sydney.*

RIGHT *Even without a garden, apartment dwellers can always find a little patch of sunshine in Sydney.*

ABOVE *City landscape designers display touches of ingenuity in their ability to find a spot for garden luxuries in amongst the high-rise dwellings.*

RIGHT *Apartment homes fronting the harbour invariably have their own boat jetties. The newer buildings come in a variety of architectural styles but they are still designed to make the most of the Australian outdoor lifestyle.*

LEFT 'Yaralla', Dame Eadith Walker Hospital, is located beside the Parramatta River in the suburb of Concord, not far from Homebush, the site of the Sydney Olympics. The old house is now a medical training centre.

OPPOSITE The Parramatta River winds its way from the harbour, around the islands of Spectacle and Cockatoo and under the Gladesville Bridge, which connects Drummoyne to Huntleys Point. The river then continues its path to the western suburbs.

ABOVE Throughout Sydney there are numerous golf courses, including The Lakes near Sydney Airport where the Greg Norman Classic is held annually.

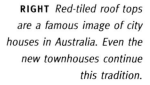

RIGHT Red-tiled roof tops are a famous image of city houses in Australia. Even the new townhouses continue this tradition.

ABOVE *Nothing sparkles quite as brightly as the evening lights around the harbour. Their multi-hued colours and shimmering reflections on the water turn Sydney into a magical realm.*

RIGHT *At night, the sleek modern lines of the monorail stations in Darling Harbour exude an ethereal glow.*

OPPOSITE *Sydney is a town that almost never sleeps. Throughout the night, traffic streams down William Street, near Kings Cross, towards the city.*

Tasmania is the second major island that makes up the continent of Australia, and its capital, Hobart, was the second city to be established under European rule. The island state is separated from the mainland by Bass Strait, which flows between it and Victoria, while being connected at the same time by an ocean shelf, where the ridges of the Great Dividing Range run underwater between the two landmasses.

Tasmania was sighted in 1642 by Abel Tasman, who called it Van Diemen's Land after the Governor-General of the Dutch East Indies. It was subsequently visited by French explorers—Marion du Fresne in 1772 and Tobias Furneaux in 1773. In 1770, the island was proclaimed a British possession by Captain James Cook along with the eastern seaboard of the mainland, all of which he charted as one continuous coastline. Cook's claim, however, did not prevent French explorers from visiting the area again. In 1792–3, Bruni d'Entrecasteaux and Huon de Kermadec named the Entrecasteaux Channel, the Huon River, Bruny Island and Recherche Bay. Nicolas Baudin also made an expedition to Tasmania in 1802, after George Bass and Matthew Flinders had established in 1798–9 that Tasmania was a separate island. Baudin's visit alarmed the British and a settlement was established within a year.

The first British party stepped ashore at Risdon Cove on the eastern shore of the Derwent River. In charge was Lieutenant John Bowen and his group numbered 49, of which 35 were convicts. In February 1804, 262 people under the leadership of Lieutenant-Governor David Collins moved to Sullivan's Cove on the western shore. The name that Bowen had given his camp at Risdon Cove, Hobart Town, was taken over by Collins' settlement and the city

HOBART

The European history of the island is a bloody and sad one. Not only were the convicts cruelly treated, the Aboriginal tribes that inhabited the land were completely annihilated. It is hard to imagine this sordid past when viewing the graceful Georgian buildings, green pastures, roaring rivers and majestic mountains that attract visitors from the mainland and all around the world.

Hobart has a population of around 200,000, its suburbs spreading around the wide reach of the Derwent River, which is crossed by the long, sweeping arch of the Tasman Bridge. The city's full glory can be viewed from Mount Wellington, which offers a dramatic backdrop to the city. A gentle air surrounds this graceful place. Among its many attractions are stone warehouses and cottages, which recall the days when Hobart was a shipbuilding centre and whaling town, visited by ships from around the world.

ABOVE *Wrest Point Hotel–Casino is located on the southern side of Sandy Bay, south of the city. The 64-metre high tower block has a revolving restaurant on the top level which offers expansive views of the city and suburbs. Wrest Point was also Australia's first legal casino.*

LEFT *The intersection of Murray and Macquarie streets is lined with grand old buildings made from local sandstone. These include St David's Cathedral, the Treasury building opposite, and a row of terraces on the other side of the road, once the site of Hobart's first gaol. This whole area has been described as one of the finest townscapes in Australia. Just down the road is the green Parliament Square.*

RIGHT *Hobart's city centre extends towards Constitution and Victoria docks at Sullivan's Cove. On the right side of Sullivan's Cove is Battery Point where the vibrant Salamanca Place markets can be found. The Place's old sandstone dockside storage buildings and large trees create a tranquil and genteel atmosphere.*

ABOVE *The piles that support the long piers of the Tasman Bridge reach heights of 81 metres. In January 1975, the bridge was hit by the bulk carrier* Lake Illawarra, *which caused two piers and three spans to collapse. Twelve people were killed, five of whom were in cars crossing the bridge. The bridge was then closed for repairs until October 1977.*

The Tasman Bridge opened in 1964 and links the city with the eastern shore of the Derwent. On the city side the three level interchange at the Queen's Domain leads to two major highways, the Tasman and the Midland.

ABOVE *The grand Government House, completed in 1858, is magnificently set in the Queen's Domain near the Tasman Bridge. The English Tudor-Gothic building has an astonishing seventy rooms and fifty chimneys.*

ABOVE *To the north of Government House is Hobart's Royal Botanical Gardens, while to the west is the cricket ground. The northern and western suburbs of Hobart are slowly expanding up the lower slopes of Mt Wellington.*

LEFT *Hobart's northern suburbs are well served with two golf courses set in natural bushland.*

BELOW *The older suburbs of Hobart have been lovingly looked after through the decades.*

FOLLOWING PAGES *Moonlight over the Derwent River highlights the beauty of Hobart's stunning location.*

LEFT *The hillside houses on the lower slopes of Mt Wellington behind Salamanca Place appear terraced. Hobart has many picturesque suburbs.*

During the seventeenth and eighteenth centuries, there were a number of sightings of the Western Australian coastline by Europeans. The first known landing took place in 1616, when Dutch explorer Dirck Hartog visited the Shark Bay region. In 1688 and again in 1699, the English adventurer William Dampier visited the north-west coast. Reports from both captains were unfavourable, and the region attracted little interest in terms of colonisation.

In 1697, Dutch sea explorer Willem de Vlamingh discovered and named the Swan River after he spotted black swans on the waterway. Some 130 years later, Britain claimed formal possession of the western side of New Holland, the name given to the continent by Abel Tasman in 1644. The first British settlement was established in 1826, in the south-west at King George Sound, but it failed. The next attempt took place in 1829. On 2 May, under the stewardship of Captain James Stirling, a party of 68 settlers landed on Rottnest Island. They moved onto the mainland on 18 June before finally deciding on the location where Perth now stands on 12 August.

PERTH

Free settlers were actively encouraged to join the colony but the transportation of Britain's 'unwanted people' to these western shores did not cease until 1868. Most of the stone buildings from Perth's early days were constructed by these convict labourers and

the city's fortunes have since ebbed and flowed according to the health of the state's businesses. Western Australia flourished during the gold rush of the 1890s and continued mining activities attract many investors.

ABOVE *The land upon which the interchange for the Narrows Bridge was built is reclaimed from the Swan River.*

OPPOSITE *The Mitchell Freeway winds its way towards the city. The train line in the middle of the two carriageways makes full use of the arterial road.*

From the small handful of early settlers Perth has expanded to 1.3 million residents. Today, the city has a comfortable mix of the old and new, with early stone buildings not looking out of place next to large, modern office blocks. The lifestyle of the city's residents is relaxed and easygoing, and as the city is located on the Swan River, with easy access to the port of Fremantle, watersports have become a way of life—for the first time in 143 years, the America's Cup was raced outside of the United States in Fremantle in 1987. Perth is also noted for its superb beaches, parks and sunny climate.

OPPOSITE *Perth's city is built in the shape of a rectangle. St George's Terrace and Murray and Wellington streets run east to west. Milligan, King, William, Barrack and Pier streets run north to south.*

ABOVE *Perth is noted for its extensive landscaped parklands. The city is built for pleasure with bicycle and walking tracks making the most of the river foreshore.*

OPPOSITE & BELOW *The Burswood Resort Hotel and Casino has a very high-tech appearance, which is softened by its 18-hole golf course.*

RIGHT *This memorial is in Kings Parks. Kings Park lies to the west of the Narrows Bridge. The park is Perth's pride and joy, it comprises 400 hectares of natural bushland which overlooks the city.*

ABOVE *Many of Australia's oldest schools and institutions are housed in grand old buildings, such as this one in Perth's eastern suburbs.*

LEFT *A number of hotels take advantage of Perth's popular northern shoreline, which is washed by the Indian Ocean.*

ABOVE *Perth's coastal suburbs are sometimes lucky enough to have waterways running nearby. They make picturesque settings for homes.*

OPPOSITE *The Barrack Street jetty provides a ferry link between the suburbs and the city. The esplanade near the jetty and the city is the venue for many festive events.*

LEFT *The Narrows Interchange lights up the city's foreshore throughout the night and the freeway looks especially magical as the bridge crosses the Swan River.*

TOP *The fading sunlight, illuminating the tall skyscrapers of Perth, accentuates the city's futuristic look.*

ABOVE *Perth's majestic skyline is silhouetted against a golden glow, which heralds the end of another fabulous day.*

I n 1831, when Captain Collet Barker was surveying the head of Gulf St Vincent, he went ashore and climbed to the top of Mount Lofty. From that vantage point he envisaged a city being built on the alluvial plain that lay between the gently curving Mount Lofty Ranges and the gulf. He could not have imagined how graceful that city would become or how it would grow to a population of just over one million people.

ADELAIDE

The plain was originally home to the Kaurna Aborigines. The first sighting of the coastline recorded in European history was in the logs of the Dutch ship *Guilden Zeepaard* in 1627. In 1792, French explorer Bruni d'Entrecasteaux sailed to the head of the Great Australian Bight, and in 1800 Englishman Lieutenant James Grant charted the coastline in the *Lady Nelson*, the first ship to pass through the Bass Strait on a voyage from London. In 1802, while surveying the coastline, Matthew Flinders came across the French explorer Nicolas Baudin at Encounter Bay. This was the incident that galvanised the British into colonising Van Diemen's Land because they believed the French were preparing to send a party to settle the island.

It was not until Charles Sturt completed his epic trip down the Murray River to Gulf St Vincent in 1830 that any real interest in South Australia began. In July 1836, five years after Barker explored the area,

ABOVE *In 1871, this elegant palm house was dismantled in Germany and each pane individually packed before shipment to Adelaide's Botanic Gardens.*

BELOW *There are many churches throughout Adelaide, earning the city its sobriquet, 'City of Churches'.*

OPPOSITE *Adelaide Bridge, one of three major bridges, connects the city's northern suburbs with the centre.*

the first party of settlers arrived at Kangaroo Island. This settlement differed to all the others in Australia as the people were all free settlers.

When the colony's Surveyor-General, Colonial William Light, arrived, the settlers moved to the mainland, near where the beachside suburb of Glenelg is now located. Light then surveyed a site six miles inland on the Torrens River and succeeded in winning approval from Captain John Hindmarsh, who had been appointed the first Governor and was en route to his new posting. Hindmarsh arrived in December 1836 and proclaimed the province, and South Australia remained part of New South Wales until 1842.

Light's vision heavily influenced the shape and feel of the modern, cosmopolitan Adelaide. As well as choosing the location, he planned the city grid so that it would be surrounded by parklands. He made a feature of the river, which winds its way north of the city centre. Today, a number of important venues flank this waterway, such as the Festival Centre, where the biennial Adelaide Arts Festival is held; the Botanic Gardens; the Zoological Gardens; the university; and the Adelaide Cricket Oval and other sports grounds. Adelaide is often called the 'City of Churches', and its many churches along with old stone cottages echo the gentle, graceful ambience of the city's early days.

OPPOSITE *The centre of Adelaide is not large in area, and like many Australian cities tall, modern skyscrapers tower over the older buildings.*

ABOVE *The streets of Adelaide were planned as a grid to be surrounded by parkland. The railway lines run along the city's northern border and Currie Street cuts through Light Square, which honours the first surveyor-general.*

RIGHT *The Adelaide Festival and Arts Centre was opened in 1973. The forecourt displays many works of art and the complex includes a concert hall and three theatres.*

LEFT *The pod-like Bicentennial Conservatory in the Botanic Gardens houses an incredible tropical rainforest.*

OPPOSITE *A footbridge runs over the Torrens River between the University of Adelaide and Grundy Gardens. The campus of the university is ten hectares and the faculties are housed in many fine old buildings.*

ABOVE *The sixteen-hectare Adelaide Botanic Gardens is picturesquely set in the north-west of the city. The gardens feature many Australian and exotic plants.*

RIGHT *Government House was built in the Regency style and is one of the many graceful buildings that line Adelaide's North Terrace.*

ABOVE *Larg's Bay lies north of Port Adelaide. Its jetty juts into Gulf St Vincent, which creates a natural western border to the greater Adelaide region.*

LEFT *The Adelaide Oval lies north of the Torrens River, opposite the distinctive white Festival and Arts Centre. It is a wonderful venue for cricket and football matches.*

TOP RIGHT *The visitors centre near the Mt Lofty fire tower is a superb location from which to view Adelaide and the gulf shoreline.*

RIGHT *The cemetery in West Parklands has devoted a whole section to servicemen who died in battle.*

FOLLOWING PAGES *The best place to see the whole of Adelaide is from Mt Lofty. At night fall the view is even more spectacular.*

The second largest city in Australia today, Melbourne's rapid rise within the colony began when a huge influx of people and capital poured into the area during the gold rush of the mid-1800s. The city centre is located on the lower reaches of the Yarra River at the head of Port Phillip Bay. It took many years of failed attempts, farcical treaties and defiance towards bureaucracy before the city was surveyed and named in 1837, after the Prime Minster of England of the day.

The coastline of Victoria was explored between 1797 and 1802, when the region, known as the Port Phillip District, was part of New South Wales. In 1803, David Collins was sent to establish a convict settlement at Port Phillip. They landed on the Mornington Peninsula but Collins felt the area was unsuitable. He was then granted permission to move his party to Tasmania and the only Europeans to visit the region for the next twenty-odd years were whalers and sealers.

MELBOURNE

In the meantime, free settlers, moving south from Sydney, had reached as far as the Murrumbidgee River by the time Hamilton Hume and William Hovell had completed their overland trek to Port Phillip at the end of 1824. Hume and Hovell reported finding 'good pastures', but they had mistaken the locality of their journey's end. They thought they had reached Westernport, and because of this error of direction those 'good pastures' at Port Phillip remained untilled for another ten years as free settlers headed for Westernport instead.

In 1827, John Batman applied for, and was refused permission by the administration in Sydney to set up land deals in the Port Phillip area. By 1834, Edward Henty decided to defy the government and moved in, occupying the area west of Portland Bay on the south coast. Batman quickly followed and established his depot at Port Phillip Bay. He then claimed to have struck a deal with local Wuywurrung people for 240,000 hectares, but this 'treaty' was ruled null and void by the government. Other settlers followed and within a year approval for settlement was granted.

Port Phillip was an immediate success. By 1843, the region had become self-supporting with both capital and labour arriving direct from the United Kingdom rather than through Sydney. A magistrate was appointed in 1836, but it was not until 1 July 1951, that Victoria was proclaimed a separate colony. The gold rush increased the city's population and despite a depression at the turn of century, Melbourne remained a financial and industrial force within Australia. After Federation, rivalry between Sydney and Melbourne as to which city would be the nation's capital was intense. This led to the establishment of Canberra, but Melbourne won the right to house the Federal Parliament until it moved to Canberra in 1927. Today, more than three million people reside in Melbourne. It is an elegant city with the statuesque architecture of the gold rush era echoed in the modern city buildings.

OPPOSITE TOP *It is impossible to mistake the international shopping complex of Daimaru in amongst all the other high-rise buildings.*

OPPOSITE BOTTOM *Melbourne is beautifully surrounded by parks and gardens.*

BELOW *Government House stands regally between the Royal Botanic Gardens with its Ornamental Lake and Kings Domain.*

ABOVE *As the dawn light bounces off the city buildings, trains begin pulling into the oldest metropolitan station in Australia, Flinders Street beside the Yarra River.*

LEFT *Beyond the gold-lit buildings, Princes Bridge and city rail lines are the gentle curves of the Dandenong Ranges.*

OPPOSITE *Some of Melbourne's tall buildings retain the elegant and imposing style of the buildings constructed during the gold rush era.*

TOP LEFT *Everybody in Melbourne seems to play sports and the old colonial establishments continue to maintain beautiful ovals.*

ABOVE *The eye-catching spire of the Victorian Arts Centre indicates the way to performance venues and the National Gallery of Victoria.*

OPPOSITE *Tree-lined Collins Street is one of the major roads in the city. At the end is the Treasury Gardens, home of the Old Treasury Building.*

ABOVE *The hallowed Melbourne Cricket Ground started life as the stadium for the 1956 Olympics.*

ABOVE LEFT *Taking time out from the stress of work, these Victorians, like the rest of country's residents, lap up the Australian sunshine.*

ABOVE *A bicycle and foot passage ramp allows access to the banks of the Yarra River, which runs through the heart of the city.*

LEFT *Melbourne is often called the 'cultural capital' of Australia, and its many parks, gardens and squares display works of art.*

ABOVE LEFT *Melbourne is now the only city in Australia which uses tram transport for commuter traffic. The trams traverse the city streets and link them to the suburbs.*

LEFT *Whether by tram, car, bicycle, foot or horse-drawn carriage, the Princes Bridge is an elegant route across the Yarra.*

BELOW LEFT *The roofs of the platforms at Flinders Street Station barely hide the trains ready to set forth to the city suburbs.*

TOP *The Royal Botanic Gardens boasts some of the best landscaping in the world, including the reposeful Ornamental Lakes.*

ABOVE *The old inner city suburbs of Melbourne retain a touch of grandeur. Some even have backyard lawn tennis courts.*

RIGHT *The Bay suburbs of Melbourne line the expansive Port Phillip and the residents live within easy reach of 97 kilometres of beaches.*

OPPOSITE *The glittering nightlife of Melbourne has lots to offer. Melbourne is 'restaurant city', and for those nightowls that want late-night entertainment there is also the opulent Crown Casino.*

ABOVE *By night the riverside walkways are lit up so that romantic evening strolls are made all the more special.*

RIGHT *The roof line of the 1880 Exhibition Buildings displays the grandeur of old Melbourne money.*

BELOW *By night, Flinders Street Station and its platforms have an otherworldly feel about them. Trains continue to operate into the small hours of the morning.*

B risbane's suburbs extend in all directions from the banks of the Brisbane River, a broad, winding waterway with many reaches, and up the hillsides, which surround the city. These natural features give the sunny capital a beautiful setting. Brisbane has an equitable climate and on a warm, sunny day in winter it is very easy to forget what chilly weather is like. Most of the city's residents wouldn't live anywhere else; as the Queensland travel slogan goes: the state is 'Beautiful one day, perfect the next!'

BRISBANE

By the time the first Europeans arrived in Australia, most of the east coast of Queensland and parts of the Gulf of Carpentaria had been charted. Not long after colonisation there were a number of forays by explorers into the north of the country, most notably John Oxley who discovered and named the Brisbane River in December 1823. It is believed that the area around Moreton Bay was then home to the Ngundanbi and Yagara Aborigines.

Oxley returned the following year with Lieutenant Henry Miller to establish a settlement. They first set up camp at Redcliffe Point at Moreton Bay, now a suburb of the city, on 24 September, 1823. Because of a lack of fresh water, the settlement was forced to move just three months later to a site on the Brisbane River, where North Quay is now located. The city, like the river, was named after Sir Thomas Brisbane, who was the Governor of New South Wales at that time.

RIGHT *Dwarfed by tall city buildings, Customs House on the waterfront was built between 1886 and 1889 by John Petrie, after whom the bight of the river at this junction is named.*

ABOVE *Brisbane's Botanic Gardens monopolises one of the best locations in the city. It is sited south of the city at the point where the river does a u-turn. The garden comprises eighteen hectares of sub-tropical plants, lakes, bicycle paths, a restaurant and a music bowl.*

Many free settlers were looking for land within the colony, so the New South Wales administration began selling freehold titles for Moreton Bay plots in December 1842. A year later, a regular sea passage service was running between Brisbane and Sydney. In 1859, Queensland was proclaimed a separate colony and Sir George Bowen was appointed the first Governor. At the time the city had a population of 23,520 people.

Rapid economic growth and an influx of people to the northern colony meant that by 1880 the population had risen to 211,040. Today there are nearly 1.5 million people calling Brisbane home, making the city the third largest in Australia. The state is also home to a thriving tourist industry, its main attractions are along the coastline and include the Great Barrier Reef, the nearby Gold Coast, its hilly hinterland with subtropical forests, and an outback that is easily accessible by good roads.

OPPOSITE *Brisbane's central business district crowds into a small plot between the bend of the river. The city is often referred to as 'a big country town'.*

ABOVE *While the actual city may be small, the whole of Greater Brisbane makes it the second largest city in the world.*

RIGHT *The Riverside Centre is the scene of lively weekend markets and a bustling nightlife because of its many restaurants.*

LEFT *The Brisbane River is crossed by seven bridges. The quaint William Jolly Bridge is the oldest, built in 1930. It was named after Brisbane's first mayor.*

BELOW *The Captain Cook Bridge feeds the traffic of the Riverside Expressway to and from the city. Further north is the Victoria Bridge, which crosses to the South Bank Parklands, the William Jolly and the Merivale, a train bridge.*

RIGHT *The Story Bridge, which runs from Kangaroo Point to the north of the city has the deepest foundations of any bridge in the world. One of its pylons sinks 40.2 metres below ground.*

OPPOSITE *Traffic from the Victoria Bridge flows between South Brisbane and Queen Street in the city centre. Queen Street is Brisbane's main shopping thoroughfare.*

LEFT *Southbank Parklands was the site of Brisbane World Expo in 1988. It was once an old residential suburb which has been revitalised into an extensive leisure complex, which runs the length of the South Brisbane Reach.*

RIGHT *The Broadwalk at Southbank is home to many restaurants offering international and Australian cuisine. It has wonderful views across the river to Gardens Point at the end of the Botanical Gardens.*

ABOVE *The artificial beach at Southbank lends a tropical feel to the complex. The beach is complete with life guards in summer and the shops nearby are fronted by colourful umbrellas, which shade the market stalls operating on Sundays.*

ABOVE *Brisbane has retained many of its early colonial buildings, but these are sometimes overshadowed by the modern glass office blocks that grace the city's skyline.*

D arwin, the administrative capital of the Northern Territory, is located on a peninsula that marks the entrance to Port Darwin. Because of its location in the north of the country, the city is considered Australia's doorway to the world. It is thought that this coastline provided the entry point for the Aborigines when they arrived in the country. Certainly there is evidence that Malay and Macassan fisherman visited the coast long before Europeans. Even today, people still arrive at this northern doorstep by boat in the hope of receiving refugee status.

The Territory's coastline was one of the first areas of the continent to be mapped by the early explorers. In 1644, twenty-one years after the Dutch ship *Arnhem* had sighted the land, Abel Tasman charted the coastline and even landed at the mouth of the Victoria River near the Western Australia border. In 1803, Matthew Flinders surveyed the coastline, but it took until 1818, when Phillip Parker King explored the area, for map makers to realise that Melville Island was not part of the mainland.

DARWIN

When the British tried to settle in the area they found the land to be less than hospitable. In 1824, Captain J.J. Bremer established a base at Fort Dundas, which lasted only four years. In 1827, Captain James Stirling surveyed the area and in 1828 Captain Collet Barker arrived at Raffles Bay with a detachment of the 39th Regiment. Stirling abandoned the site two years later but in 1838, Bremer again tried to form a permanent settlement, this time at Port Essington. This settlement lasted until December 1849, and during that time the *Beagle*, the ship made famous by Charles Darwin's epic voyages, docked at the settlement in July 1839. A crew member, Lieutenant John Stokes, discovered a large bay in

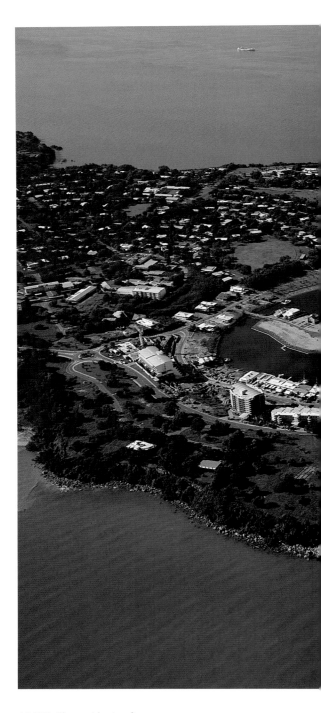

ABOVE *The residents of Darwin enjoy not one, but three still waterways: Frances, Darwin and Fannie.*

OPPOSITE *The Diamond Beach Casino is the centre of Darwin's nightlife. It is wonderfully situated on the edge of Mindil Beach.*

FOLLOWING PAGES *The city centre of Darwin faces south-west, fronting the port of the same name.*

the south and the ship's captain J.C. Wickham named it Darwin Bay after the renowned botanist. At the time the area was occupied by the Laragiya Aborigines. It took another thirty years before G.W. Goyder, the Surveyor-General for South Australia, was sent with a party in 1869 to plan the site for a town. The new settlement was known as Palmerston, and it was not officially called Darwin until 1911.

Darwin's turbulent history brought many changes to the city skyline over the years. When the Overland Telegraph Line was completed in 1872, Darwin became the nation's link to the world via a submarine cable to Java. The gold rushes at Pine Creek brought a large influx of people to the area. During the Second World War, Darwin's military and airforce bases attracted the attention of the Japanese, who bombed the city on 19 February 1942, razing the town and causing 243 deaths. Immediately, the city was evacuated of civilians, and the whole town had to be entirely rebuilt after the war. The most recent devastation to Darwin was on Christmas Day in

1974, when Cyclone Tracey hit, leaving only four hundred buildings intact. Darwin was again rebuilt, and since that time the city has taken on a whole new lease of life.

Today, the capital of the Northern Territory has a population of nearly 80,000, comprising an amazing cross-section of people. A visit to Mindil Beach when the markets are in full swing reveals the city's great cultural diversity. This tropical capital city is also an inspiration to many artists and photographers, particularly when the sun goes down in a blaze of colour over Fannie Bay.

OPPOSITE *Darwin differs from the other Australian cities, in that the orderly streets are lined with modern, low-rise buildings, built since Cyclone Tracey struck in 1974.*

ABOVE *Palm trees lend a tropical feel to this most northern of Australian cities. Even the modern shopping centres have a relaxed, easygoing feel.*

RIGHT *Darwin's Parliament House has all the grandeur of an ancient Greek building, yet it is a recent addition to the cityscape.*

ABOVE *There are few high-rise buildings in Darwin, and those that stretch beyond three floors are often hotels.*

ABOVE RIGHT *The tree-lined city streets are wide enough to accommodate cars parked on an angle.*

OPPOSITE *The main street of Darwin is called Smith. It runs parrallel to Port Darwin. Like many of Australia's capital cities, Darwin has a shopping mall in the centre, where the only traffic is on foot.*

LEFT *One of the few buildings to survive Darwin's devastations was Seven Gables, the Administrator's House. Located near Fort Point, the house has expansive views of the port.*

BELOW *Modern hotel accommodation with boat moorings make the most of the northern waters.*

RIGHT *Houses in the suburbs of Darwin are beautifully planned so that each has plenty of space. After the wet season the city erupts in glorious shades of green*

OPPOSITE *Darwin's population is ever-increasing as residents from other Australian cities search for a more tranquil place to live. Even Darwin's newer suburbs are landscaped to create picturesque surroundings.*

I n the Southern Tablelands of New South Wales lies the Australian Capital Territory, home of the national capital, Canberra. The city's name comes from the Aboriginal word canberry, which has been translated as 'meeting place'—the local people used to gather here to feast on Bogong moths that migrate annually to the nearby Brindabella Range. The area was first recorded in European history in 1820, when Charles Smith, James Vaughan and Joseph Wild camped by a river they called Fish, now known as the Molonglo. The explorer Alan Cunningham reported in 1824 that the area had good soil, and before long pastoralists were staking their claims.

CANBERRA

When the states formed a federation in 1901, there was much debate over where the future federal capital should be located. When the present area was agreed upon and signed over to the Federal Parliament in 1908, it became the only major city in Australia to be built inland, some 150 kilometres from the coast. The land package included Jervis Bay, so that the city could have a federal port. However, as road, rail and air transport soon became the major means of transport, Jervis Bay has been used in an official capacity only by the Royal Australian Naval College.

A competition for the design of the city was launched in 1911 and the first prize went to an American architect, Walter Burley Griffin. His entry, supported by beautiful drawings by his future wife, Marion Mahony, divided the city into sections laid out carefully in a system of land and water axes. Construction for the new city, to be built on the open, undulating countryside, began on 12 March, 1913. The central focus of Canberra's layout is Parliament House, sited on Capital Hill.

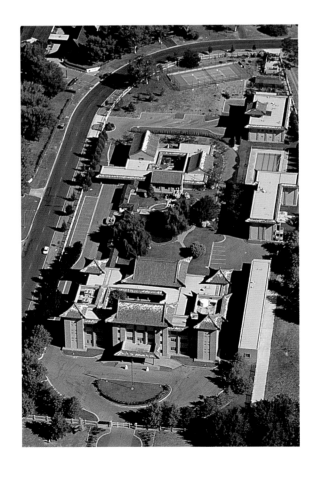

OPPOSITE TOP
Roundabouts play an important role in the movement of traffic through Canberra. The city has few traffic lights in comparison to other major metropolises.

OPPOSITE BOTTOM *The suburbs of Barton, Forrest and Yarralumla, which surround Parliament House, form an 'embassy belt'. Like the Chinese Embassy, most of the official consulate residences reflect their country's architectural style.*

ABOVE *Beyond the Captain Cook Memorial Jet is Parliament House. The Tidbinbilla and Brindabella ranges surround the city.*

Once called the 'bush capital', Canberra is a beautiful, modern city with broad, tree-lined roads and low buildings, which do not interrupt the view of the surrounding hills. It is home to many national institutions, including the National Library, the High Court, the National Art Gallery and the Australian National University. This city is also the location of the official residences of the Governor-General and the Prime Minister and houses many overseas embassies. A large number of embassy buildings have been constructed to reflect the culture of the country they represent. The serene and regal-like Lake Burley Griffin, which was created by damming the Molonglo River, graces the city's heart and is surrounded by generous parklands, planned for the enjoyment of Canberra's 300,000 residents and many visitors.

PARLIAMENT
HOUSE

The Federal Parliament of Australia moved to its stately new headquarters (OPPOSITE) in May, 1988. Set grandly on Capital Hill, it is the focal point of the city's landscape and *raison d'être*. The top of the hill was removed during construction and the building retains the original height of the site. Lawns were grown on top to give the image that the hill is still intact. The massive flagmast (LEFT), which rises 81 metres and weighs 220 tonnes, is symbolic of the seat of power. The building is strong in Australian symbolism: the forecourt (BELOW LEFT) represents the outback and Aboriginal culture and 48 marble-clad columns in the foyer represent a eucalypt forest. The elegant old parliament house (BELOW) is now a portrait gallery.

OPPOSITE The Australian War Memorial was erected in memory of service men and women who lost their lives on battlefields.

RIGHT The National Library of Australia overlooks the lake near the Commonwealth Avenue Bridge, which leads to Capital Hill.

ABOVE The old parliament house was opened in 1927. In front of it is another building from the same era: the Edmund Barton government office building, in honour of Australia's first prime minister. By the lakeside is the High Court and National Gallery.

RIGHT Telstra Tower on Black Mountain rises 195 metres above the summit. The tower is the central communications link for the city and it also houses a viewing gallery and restaurant.

FOLLOWING PAGES The Captain Cook Memorial Jet shoots a water column up to 137 metres high. It is sited near Regatta Point. Up the rise from the point is Vernon Circle, where the buildings of Canberra's Civic Centre are located.

ABOVE *Evening light over the suburbs of Canberra lends an ethereal glow to a city that is based on politics. Canberra is idyllically sited on a plain surrounded by ranges.*

ABOVE *Lake Burley Griffin was named after the architect who designed the layout of Canberra. His design included a water axis, around which the city would be built.*

ABOVE *A golden sun set strikes Parliament House. The building contains 4500 rooms and it is primely located on Capital Hill, a site earmarked by architect Walter Burley Griffin.*

WATERWAYS

WATERWAYS

All of Australia's major cities have been built on waterways. Darwin and Sydney have extensive harbours and flowing into Sydney's famous waterway is the winding Parramatta River, fed by streams flowing east down the ridges of the Blue Mountains. Canberra is nestled around Lake Burley Griffin, created by damming the Molonglo River. Melbourne's Yarra River, the Swan in Perth, the Torrens in Adelaide, the Derwent in Hobart and the Brisbane in the Sunshine State's capital, all provide picturesque settings for tall buildings and the extensive parks and gardens that line their shores.

The Search for an Inland Sea

Before colonisation, Aboriginal communities who lived in the Sydney basin built canoes to travel around the harbour. When Europeans arrived, ships provided the only transport between Australia and other countries. At the end of Mrs Macquarie's Point in Sydney a chair is chiselled into the rock where the Governor's wife used to sit and watch the tall ships come and go. Until plane travel became more accessible in the late 1960s and early 70s, seagoing vessels remained the favoured means of transport and they docked at most of the country's major.

Coastal waterways provided an invaluable service and continue to do so. Today, all the city waterways are utilised by residents in some form or another, whether it be for pleasure or for business enterprises.

Ferries are a major commuter transport system around Sydney Harbour and along the Parramatta River. In Sydney, as well as in other larger Australian harbours and ports, huge cruise liners and cargo-carrying hulks are tugged into wharves to unload their consignments, and on most days in all the capital cities, pleasure craft can be seen bobbing on harbour, river or lake surfaces.

OPPOSITE TOP *The Carillon stands on Aspen Island in Lake Burley Griffin.*

ABOVE *Houses front the banks of Sydney's Parramatta River.*

LEFT *Sailing is popular in most city waterways, especially Sydney's harbour.*

PREVIOUS PAGES *The South Alligator River snakes across Top End floodplains.*

The primary concern of the early European inhabitants when deciding where to establish their settlements was not only water access, but also the availability of fresh water. However strange it may seem, Australia is considered the driest continent on earth, despite being literally surrounded by water. The reason is the low rainfall, which means there are few notable permanent stream or river systems.

Most of the continent is arid, and those people who don't live on the coastal plains are forced to rely, for the most part, on subterranean water supplies.

OPPOSITE *Waterfalls tumble through tropical rainforests in north Queensland.*

ABOVE *Tasmania's south-west is one of the few places in Australia to have constantly flowing rivers.*

In these instances, deep bores are sunk into the ground to reach the artesian basins. The Great Artesian Basin, which runs under much of inland Queensland, northern New South Wales and into the Northern Territory, is the largest in the world. It covers a mammoth two million square kilometres.

Of all the states, only Tasmania can claim to be moisture-laden. The state's high rainfall, coupled with the fact that the majority of the island is mostly highland, have resulted in short-running but fast-flowing rivers such as the Gordon and Franklin. The longest river in Tasmania is the Derwent, around which Hobart is located, and it runs for only 193 kilometres. Tasmania's wild rivers have been extensively harnessed in the past by state authorities to provide hydro-generated electricity. However, during the 1970s, large and sometimes violent protests were mounted against the extensive damming required to generate this power. A number of projects were cancelled in favour of preserving the island's beautiful wilderness.

In the early days rivers provided one of the few ways for explorers to travel inland. The problem was that the coastal rivers flowed eastwards down the Great Dividing Range, and the deep canyons of the eastern uplands proved to be a barrier to travelling westwards. When a route over the range was finally opened up, the early explorers became convinced that there was an inland sea because the few rivers that were discovered on the other side flowed westwards. The idea of an inland sea was also supported by the findings of Matthew Flinders when he charted the coastline. Flinders noted few river mouths around the coastline, so concluded that a continent of this size must have an inland sea for rain run-off. It wasn't until Charles Sturt's explorations of the continent's interior and his charting of Australia's largest river system, the Murray–Darling, between 1829 and 1831 that people became aware of Australia's arid outback.

The Murray–Darling river system is approximately 3500 kilometres long. The 'mighty' Murray, the longest river in Australia, makes up 2600 kilometres of that length. Its source is high in the Snowy Mountains and it provides a natural border between the states of New South Wales and Victoria before winding its final, languid 650 kilometres through South Australia to Lake Alexandrina, south of Adelaide. Flowing into the Murray are the Lachlan, Murrumbidgee and Darling, which runs a long course down the western part of New South Wales. The Darling is fed by a number of westward-flowing rivers from inland Queensland and New South Wales.

By the late-nineteenth century rivers, such as the Murray and Darling, were being utilised to transport supplies to the settlers moving further away from the cities in search of fresh pastures. However, most of the mainland's inland rivers rely on the tropical wet seasons of the north to provide their flow, and they tend to drain as quickly as they fill. If the season has had an exceptionally high rainfall, areas the size of European countries can be submerged by the downpour.

During summer, Kakadu in the Northern Territory becomes a vast wetland teeming with wildlife. The Kakadu National Park was inscribed on the World Heritage List in 1979 and its name comes from a word used by Gagudju people who live in the region. Its flood plains and lagoons are drained by the Nourlangie and Magela creeks, tributaries of the South Alligator and East Alligator rivers. Most of these streams have their source in the Arnhem Land plateau. One of the few permanent rivers in the centre is the Katherine, which carves its way through a rocky plateau and creates a spectacular gorge.

Inland Australia is also devoid of permanent lakes. Those that exist are for the most part ephemeral drainage grounds for the rivers when they do flow. Lake Eyre is the largest, and most of the time its 9323 square kilometres is simply a bed of salt and dry mud. Most of Australia's permanent lakes lie near the coast and were created either by the build-up of sand or by rising seawater entering low-lying areas, such as Lake Macquarie in New South Wales. Other types of lake to be found in Australia are glacial and volcanic crater lakes. In the Atherton Tableland of north Queensland some crater lakes are surrounded by rainforest, while in Tasmania glacial lakes are perched in the high, forbidding peaks of the south-west wilderness region.

LEFT *In summer, Kakadu National Park becomes a spectacular wetland teeming with wildlife.*

LEFT *Few harbours in the world match Sydney's in terms of size and depth. It covers 5504 hectares and plunges 47.2 metres.*

ABOVE *With some 58 wharves, such as these at the entrance to Darling Harbour, Port Jackson is Australia's most important shipping waterway. Over 3000 ships carrying 35 million tonnes of cargo berth in Sydney yearly.*

RIGHT *There are a number of islands within Port Jackson. Fort Denison, located near the Opera House, was once a holding cell for the colony's worst convicts. They called it Pinchgut in honour of the meagre rations given to them while on the island.*

Captain James Cook peered into a waterway hidden behind two sentinel-like headlands, but didn't enter. Eighteen years later, Captain Arthur Phillip sailed beyond the entrance and promptly set up camp in what he described as: "the finest harbour in the world". The ease of access to and from Port Jackson—there are two deep channels by which large ships can enter and leave—the lack of navigational hazards within, and the depth and extent of the waterway create a shipping paradise. The view from one of the harbour foreshore parks is a colourful parade of the large variety of watercraft that frequent the harbour, including water taxies (RIGHT), car ferries (BELOW), catamarans and cruise ships (BELOW RIGHT), fishing boats (OPPOSITE, TOP LEFT), sailing ships (OPPOSITE, TOP RIGHT), tall-masted ships (OPPOSITE BOTTOM) and commuter ferries (MAIN PICTURE).

HARBOUR
TRANSPORT

OPPOSITE *The Torrens River gently flows between the city centre of Adelaide and North Adelaide and is lined by delightful parks. This tranquil waterway is used often by row boats and pedal craft.*

RIGHT *The Swan River winds its way from the port of Fremantle through Perth's suburbs to its upper reaches where vineyards are located.*

BELOW *The Swan is a calm waterway that bustles with boats, from colourful sailing craft to commuter ferries.*

RIGHT *Melbourne's Yarra River is surrounded by extensive parklands, which make walking along its banks or rowing upon the water a special and idyllic experience.*

FOLLOWING PAGES *The walkway across the Yarra near Flinders Street Station and Princes Bridge allows easy pedestrian access to the waterside cafes and restaurants at South Gate.*

RIGHT *For Darwin's residents a sail along Sadgroves Creek allows a closer look at the mangrove vegetation. The creek flows into Frances Bay and beyond the headland is Port Darwin and Fannie Bay.*

LEFT *The Brisbane River rises in the Brisbane Ranges and meanders through the city before entering the sea at Moreton Bay. Large ships can dock as far as the city, but cruise and sailing ships are more often seen on the river's reaches.*

OPPOSITE *The Derwent River cuts a swathe through the valley of the same name. Hobart is located twenty kilometres from the mouth of the river, which flows into the Tasman Sea.*

LEFT *Tasmania has a number of fast-flowing rivers that carry huge volumes of water, as well as smaller ones that run off the highlands and flow quietly into the ocean.*

BELOW *The Mossman River winds through the Daintree National Park in tropical north Queensland and cruise boats are the best way to see the rainforest up close.*

LEFT *The Norman, Saxby and Leichhardt rivers reach their conclusion at the Gulf of Carpentaria. A number of small communities make full use of the gulf and its rivers for fishing.*

ABOVE *Many north Queensland rivers are lined with undisturbed rainforest and the water is so pure it is possible to see the river bed.*

RIGHT *Farms make full use of the fertile valley between the Atherton Tableland and the ocean. Rivers flow down from the range and allow for irrigation of the crops.*

LEFT *Mandurah, south of Perth in Western Australia, has become a holiday resort because the calm, protected Peel Inlet is excellent for crabbing and fishing.*

BELOW *The Fitzgerald River runs through the national park of the same name, which has been declared a biosphere reserve because of its unique and fragile ecology.*

OPPOSITE *The Murray River is Australia's longest river. As it flows from inland Victoria to South Australia it makes a languid path through the silted scrub plains.*

RIGHT *In the wet season the waters of the Fitzroy River rise so high that only the tree tops mark the river banks. The Fitzroy cuts through the Kimberley plateau in northern Western Australia, creating a number of deep gorges.*

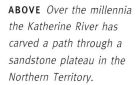

ABOVE *Over the millennia the Katherine River has carved a path through a sandstone plateau in the Northern Territory.*

RIGHT *The high walls of Katherine Gorge create a cool oasis in the tropical north. The majority of people who visit the region see the gorge by boat because the steep sides are truly spectacular.*

OPPOSITE *Three Alligator rivers cross the Northern Territory, the East, South and West. The East Alligator rises in Arnhem Land and joins its siblings at Van Diemen Gulf.*

RIGHT *The Adelaide River cuts a swathe through the plains between Darwin and Kakadu National Park. It runs for 180 kilometres.*

BELOW *Crossing the rivers of the north is near impossible during the wet season and hazardous at other times because they are infested with crocodiles.*

KAKADU WETLANDS

The World Heritage-listed Kakadu National Park borders the Aboriginal Arnhem Land reserve and includes the sandstone escarpment (OPPOSITE, FAR RIGHT) which defines the boundary. The lagoons and marshes of the park undergo a dramatic change during the wet season. Monsoonal rains fill the low-lying areas and grass can grow up to two metres tall. The whole region teems with wildlife, including 50 native animals, 43 native fish, 22 frog species and 270 species of bird, such as jabirus, long-legged brolgas, ducks, herons, parrots and honeyeaters. The park also has an incredibly rich and diverse ecosystem comprising thousands of plant species. Mangroves, grasslands, open eucalypt woodlands and patches of rainforest are all represented within its 20,000 square kilometres.

PREVIOUS PAGES *Clifton Lake is one of a chain of beautiful coastal lakes near the Yalgorup National Park, south of Perth in Western Australia.*

OPPOSITE & BELOW *Lakes, perched high in the often bleak mountains of Tasmania's south-west, formed in indentations left by the movement of glaciers.*

TOP *Lake Eacham and Lake Barrine were formed over 10,000 years ago by blasts of water forced through the earth's surface by lava. Today, they are tranquil settings surrounded by rainforests.*

ABOVE *Lake Macquarie lies north of Sydney and is popular with holiday-makers and fishermen.*

RANGES AND FORESTS

RANGES AND FORESTS

D ry, barren, flat: three uninspiring words used often to describe the continent of Australia, yet the geographic and climatic conditions that convey meaning to these words have contributed to a uniquely beautiful landscape. The lack of rain has resulted in a flora that can withstand drought conditions. Australia just wouldn't be the same without the ubiquitous gum tree. Mineral-rich Western Australia has some of the world's oldest surface rock, some dating from the Archaean era 3800 million years ago. The red flat image of the inland is possible only because millions of years of erosion and little volcanic activity during the past 1400 years have resulted in a land surface that has not buckled in the same way as other continents.

Monumental Citadels

Despite all these characteristics, these three words can be refuted as well. There are areas of the continent which receive sufficient rainfall to enable thick forests to grow, such as the rainforests of north Queensland and the wilderness regions of Tasmania. Additionally, the continent has an amazing array of flora and fauna. The country's isolation from other landforms over the past sixty million years has resulted in species found nowhere else in the world. With the arrival of humans to the continent, new plants and animals have been introduced, rapidly

OPPOSITE TOP *The brilliant red Initiation Rock lies in the middle of a valley surrounded by cliffs. It is an important Aboriginal site in the Northern Territory's Finke Gorge National Park.*

OPPOSITE BOTTOM *The plants in Australia attract considerable scientific interest because of their development in isolation from other countries.*

ABOVE *A mist-shrouded cascade plunges off the steeply eroded cliffs into the forested Grose Valley in the Blue Mountains.*

expanding the country's ecological structures. It is a mistake, also, to think of Australia as without uplands; flat though much of the continent is, there are major upland areas in all the states and territories.

The Great Dividing Range is the most prominent of all the upland regions and it is often described as the 'backbone' of the country. It is actually a series of ranges, rather than just one, running southwards from Cape York Peninsula and ending in Tasmania. Towards the south of the mainland it forks westwards into Victoria to create the Grampians and southwards to travel underwater, forming part of the continental shelf, before resurfacing in the 'apple isle'. The most notable feature of the range is the steep, dissected cliffs on its eastern slopes. The steep, rugged inclines were eroded out of a large sandstone plateau and they occur from just north of Cairns to almost as far south as the New South Wales and Victorian border.

It was these sheer box-shaped canyons that prevented early European explorers from moving inland. The first passage over the range was discovered at the Blue Mountains, west of Sydney. Like most of the range, the Blue Mountains is covered in trees, with the sheer cliffs plunging into heavily forested valleys. The area takes its name from the blue haze that surrounds the range when viewed from a distance, a phenomenon caused by the distillation of eucalypt oil.

All along the range land suitable for farming was discovered on plateaux. South of Sydney lies the Southern Tablelands, atop the Illawarra Escarpment. In the north, the rich plains of the Darling Downs were first reached by Allan Cunningham in 1827, when he found the gap in the range that now bears his name. Just beyond Cairns is the equally fertile Atherton Tableland, 32,000 square kilometres of agricultural farmland. This tableland is also home to a number of country towns, pockets of rainforest and waterfalls, which tumble down off the steep slopes. The stunning rainforests of north Queensland feature often on postcards, particularly where they grow down the slopes and meet the sea at Cape Tribulation.

Almost all of Australia's highest peaks are along the Great Dividing Range, with the exception of Mount Zeil in the Northern Territory. Mount Kosciuszko in New South Wales is Australia's highest mountain.

It stands a moderate 2228 metres above sea level and was named after a Polish patriot and general by a fellow countryman, the explorer Paul Strzelecki. It is thought that Strzelecki was the first European to scale Kosciuszko when he reached the summit on 12 March 1840. Mount Kosciuszko forms part of the Australian Alps, one of the few places in the country where snow falls. During the winter months, this part of the range and the Snowy Mountains in Victoria become a playground for skiers and snowboarders.

The only state in the country to comprise substantial mountainous terrain is Tasmania. Its steep

OPPOSITE *The Barkley Tableland in the Northern Territory was uplifted by mighty geological forces thousands of years ago. The escarpment marks the boundary of Kakadu National Park.*

MacDonnell Range, where wonderful walks within steep red ravines await the traveller. The tops of these ravines also provide prime spots from which to view the flat rolling landscape of the surrounding deserts.

In the far north lies the Arnhem Land escarpment within the Kakadu National Park. Like the eastern escarpment, it marks the edge of an extensive plateau, the Barkly Tableland. In the west are the ranges of Hamersley and Kimberley, where Purnululu National Park provides protection for the eerie and unusual Bungle Bungle range. In the south of Western Australia the Stirling Range locks in a fertile pocket of land where forests of karri and jarrah trees can grow to more than forty metres tall.

Over two-thirds of Australia's forest trees are eucalypts, most of them native only to this country. These trees are evergreen and most have evolved to be resistant in part to drought and wild fires. A large portion of Australia's unique forests are protected in areas declared national or conservation parks, and some lie within World Heritage areas, such as the islands of Great Barrier Reef, the Wet Tropics of Queensland and the Tasmanian Wilderness. Such protection means that these areas can be monitored to ensure that endangered flora and fauna are given a good chance to develop naturally.

escarpments were carved by glacial activity and winter on these most southerly heights can be very bitter. In the south-west of the country is a large wilderness area, parts of which have never been explored. Here nearly 800,000 hectares of undisturbed forests have been set aside as a national park.

Ranges in the centre of country are few and far between, and little vegetation graces their slopes. The Flinders, north of Adelaide, are ancient and worn down. They are cut by deep gorges and the colours of the ranges' rockface are simply breathtaking. Further north in the Northern Territory is the red arc of the

OPPOSITE *Rainforests cover the valleys and ridges of the Great Dividing Range in north Queensland. Beyond the rise is the Atherton Tableland.*

RIGHT *Farms on the Atherton Tableland and in the coastal valleys create patchwork-like patterns across the landscape.*

RIGHT *The discovery of fertile land atop the plateaux of the Great Dividing Range boosted Australia's agricultural industry.*

FOLLOWING PAGES *One of the most picturesque sights in Australia is in the far north of Queensland where the rainforests of the Daintree National Park grow thickly down the range and meet the shoreline.*

RANGES AND FORESTS   181

ABOVE *Afternoon sunlight bathes the top of a ridge in the Blue Mountains. The multicoloured sandstone cliffs kept European expansion at bay for a quarter of a century.*

FAR LEFT *There is an incredible variety of habitats for plants in the Blue Mountains, including grasslands, heaths, swamps, woodlands and temperate rainforests.*

LEFT *The Gibraltar Range National Park encloses 15,483 hectares of rainforest-covered ridges on the New England escarpment in northern New South Wales.*

OPPOSITE *The Tidbinbilla Range creates a scenic backdrop for Canberra.*

BELOW *Pink light dapples
snow-covered peaks in the
Kosciuszko National Park.
Vegetation atop Australia's
highest peaks is less dense
than along the rest of the
Great Dividing Range.*

ABOVE *There are over five hundred eucalypt species in Australia and their habitats range from arid inland regions to high ridges, such as Ramshead near Mount Kosciuszko.*

RIGHT *The Alpine National Park protects much of the Victorian highlands in the north-east corner of the state. In spring the heathlands of the alps are covered in wildflowers.*

ABOVE *Mount Wellington overshadows Hobart. It towers 1270 metres above sea level and during the colder months of the year snow falls upon the peak.*

RIGHT *The rugged ridge-line of the Grampians in Victoria form the western rampart of the Great Dividing Range. They are composed of folded sediment rock that has eroded over the centuries.*

ABOVE *The Grampians were first explored by T.L. Mitchell in July 1936, who named the range after the Grampians in Scotland. The highest peak is Mount Williams, standing 1166 metres tall.*

ABOVE The stark, dramatic range in Tasmania's South West National Park was created in the ice age. Immense glaciers cut through the rock and left a rugged path of peaks.

RIGHT The mountains of Tasmania are composed mostly of dolerite and quartzite, both of which are resistant to erosion. The imposing summits of the ranges have remained relatively unchanged since the ice age subsided.

RIGHT *Forest clearing by tree felling and backburning is a controversial issue. For some it is a clear case of land abuse, for others it is deemed necessary to prevent the spread of wild fires and to open up new residential districts.*

ABOVE *During the ice age almost one-fifth of Tasmania was covered in ice caps, some as deep as three hundred metres. The weight and movement of these formed a number of flat and round hilltops.*

A quarry in the Adelaide Hills removes sandstone and shale for use in building and landscape gardening. Because this range provides the highest point near the city of Adelaide, it is a perfect location for television towers.

OPPOSITE *In order to create roadways over the ranges in Australia, such as this one in the Adelaide Hills district, surveyors chart the contours of the ridges and valleys to find a suitable path.*

RIGHT *A pipeline follows the natural line of the barren slopes, which run along the Fleurieu Peninsula to the south of Adelaide.*

LEFT *The vegetation on Kangaroo Island is predominately mallee scrub and dry sclerophyll. Thick forests of these plants grow in Flinders Chase National Park.*

RED PEAKS
OF THE INTERIOR

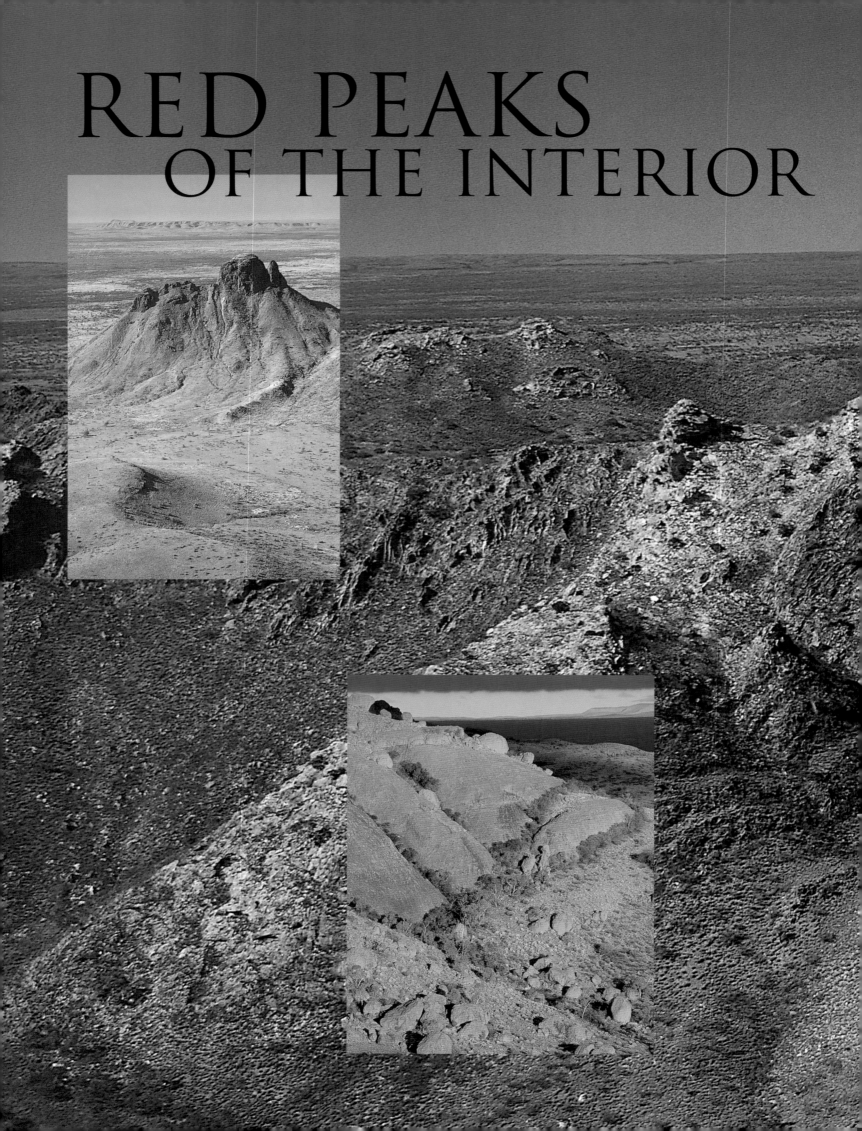

The MacDonnell Ranges arch roughly 65 kilometres to the east and 320 kilometres to the west of Alice Springs in central Australia. The sheer red peaks (MAIN PICTURE) are intersected with chasms and gorges, such as Kings Canyon (BELOW) lying south of the West MacDonnells. Its steepest side is 270 metres high. Haasts Bluff (OPPOSITE TOP) at the western end of the range was named by Ernest Giles in 1872 after a well-known New Zealand geologist and explorer. Ormiston Pound (BOTTOM) is a natural rocky amphitheatre about ten kilometres wide, located to the west of Alice Springs. Within the red peaks of the interior are pockets of lush vegetation, some relics from an eras when the area was thick with tropical vegetation. Today, the most prominent form of trees are ghost gumtrees (OPPOSITE BOTTOM), their white trunks appearing especially stark against the red rocks.

TOP *King George River carves through the ancient Kimberley Plateau in far north Western Australia.*

ABOVE *Purnululu National Park on the southern edge of the Kimberley plateau contains the mysterious Bungle Bungle Range. These beehive-like domes are extremely fragile.*

OPPOSITE *The Bungle Bungle massif is composed of sandstone lined with black lichen and orange silica, which creates the distinctive stripes.*

OUTBACK

OUTBACK

Surviving All Odds

Aboriginal communities have inhabited the centre of the mainland for hundreds of centuries and the area is still an important part of their customs and beliefs. Their Dreaming stories, which are passed onto successive generations, contain secrets about their sacred sites, such as Uluru. For vast numbers of people from all over the world these sites have also become spiritual places, where every year thousands make pilgrimage-like visits. The centre of the mainland is often referred to as the Red Heart, and it is easy to see why. This vibrant colour dominates the outback, but there is also a kaleidoscope of other colours—ochre, sand and tans along with green and white. Once Europeans had passed the ranges and forests lying near the coast they began to wonder about what lay further inland. Many turned back before completing their treks or died along the way because they were unable to cope with the harsh conditions. Having never encountered Australia's interior or any terrain resembling the outback, these early explorers were unprepared. Aboriginal groups sometimes tried to help these hapless trailblazers, but their offers were not always accepted, as in the case of Robert Burke and William Wills who died on the return journey of their famous trek in 1861 to the Gulf of Carpentaria. For the most part, what drew explorers into this inhospitable environment was the promise of riches and fame. Eager explorers wanted to be the one to discover the mythical inland sea.

PREVIOUS PAGES *The landscape surrounding Uluru is flat and dry and appears to roll on forever towards the horizon.*

OPPOSITE *The Mungo National Park in the far west of New South Wales contains the whispering sand dunes of the dry Willandra Lakes.*

ABOVE *The red weathered rocks and sparse vegetation near Kings Canyon is typical of the central inland region.*

The most successful of all the inland explorers was John MacDouall Stuart. His epic journeys during 1860–2 opened a route between Adelaide and the top end of the country and later became the path for the Overland Telegraph Line. Stuart's party made three attempts at this north–south trek before finally reaching their destination. Stuart's final trip left him weak and almost blind. He died in 1864, two months after he returned home to England. Other notable inland explorers were John Eyre, Charles Sturt, Thomas Mitchell and Burke and Wills.

Australia's deserts are harsh terrain. The arid and semi-arid zones of the outback cover almost two-thirds of the mainland. Most of the inland is lucky to receive 200 millimetres of rain a year. The average for Lake Eyre in South Australia is only about 100 millimetres. The little vegetation that grows in these areas is largely scrub, hummock or tussock grasses.

Sturts Stony Desert in the north-east corner of South Australia is a vast, desolate plain of gibbers, a Dharug Aboriginal word for the smallish, flint-like stones that cover the region. The Simpson, in the centre, covers a large 780,000 square kilometres and consists mainly of long red sand ridges.

Other spectacular inland sights include the fragile sand sweeps at Willandra, the haunting Pinnacles at Nambung National Park in Western Australia, and the white sand dunes at Ceduna in South Australia, near the Nullarbor Plains. Perhaps the image that comes to most people's mind when they think about the outback is Uluru (Ayers Rock).

Uluru was not discovered by Europeans until 1873, when William Gosse made an expedition west of the MacDonnell Ranges. The rock was created when the seas covered the inland regions. It is composed of sand and gravel that was compacted by the waters of the Pre-Cambrian age almost six hundred million years ago. Incredible geological forces turned the rock ninety degrees so that it protruded above the land surface. Uluru stands almost 335 metres above the ground but the vast majority of its mass lies underground.

Nearby, the striking red, rounded forms of Kata Tjuta (The Olgas) are of the same geological composition as Uluru. The colouring of all these rocks is believed to be caused by the red sands of the desert being perpetually blown onto them. Kata Tjuta means 'many heads' in the local Aboriginal language, which refers to their form.

The shape of Kata Tjuta is similar to that of the Bungle Bungle Range in Purnululu National Park

ABOVE *Shrouded in mist the weathered domes of Kata Tjuta, located not far from Uluru, appear even more magical. The name given to this collection of huge boulders by the Aborigines, Kata Tjuta, means 'many heads'. It is not difficult to see why.*

on the Kimberley Plateau in Western Australia. These massifs have been weathered into striped domes, which is why they are often described as beehive-shaped.

Despite its isolation, many people live in the outback and towns continue to flourish. The outback town that most people know about is Alice Springs, made famous by the television mini-series based on the Neville Shute book, *A Town Like Alice*. The Alice is surrounded by the MacDonnell Ranges and has been the centre of inland communication since the Overland Telegraph Line was established. Originally called Stuart after the explorer, the town was surveyed in 1888 and renamed in 1933. Today, the town has a population of nearly 25,000.

In the age of airline travel, satellite television and the internet, the outback is not as isolated as it once was, yet it would be rash to underestimate its harshness—from time to time travellers in the region do fail to return. Water is scarce on most of the continent, particularly in the outback. There are cool oases within the dry parched land but you need to know where to find them, especially when temperatures climb to over 40 degrees Celsius. Travellers must be properly equipped, but this difficult terrain between the continent's extremities—3138 kilometres north–south between Cape York and South Cape, and 3983 kilometres west–east between Steep Point and Cape Byron—is rich in wonderful sights.

ABOVE *Farming beyond the fertile coastal plains is made possible by bore water and irrigation. Wheatfields have been planted near Mintaro in South Australia.*

RIGHT *One of the mainstays of inland industry is sheep grazing. Shearers have been immortalised in Australian ballads, such as* Click Go the Shears.

RIGHT *On the edges of the dry outback there are fertile valleys, like the Barossa, where agricultural ventures thrive. The Barossa valley is famous for its vineyards.*

BELOW *Cattle droving is an enterprise which has successfully used the vast inland region. Ranches, such as this one in Central Queensland, can be as large in area as some European countries.*

OPPOSITE *The railhead near the Kulgera Roadhouse is an important link in the long trek between Adelaide and Darwin. The line travels through the central outback region.*

RIGHT *Cars travelling through the outback need to be sturdy and reliable. The wet season brings torrential downpours which can block road travel to some communities for long periods of time.*

ABOVE *Large trucks are still an essential means of transporting heavy farm equipment, especially for stations that do not have rail access.*

RIGHT *The small community of Cooinda in the Northern Territory typifies outback towns. The buildings are often simple structures that look makeshift.*

ABOVE *The controversial Rangers Uranium Mine is located within the Kakadu National Park. Its treatment plant is the largest in the world.*

RIGHT *Many protests erupted over the establishment of Rangers, but the region is rich in orebody and applications for more mines are under consideration.*

ULURU

Called Ayers Rock by William Gosse in 1873, Uluru is a majestic sight that symbolises the outback of Australia. This monolith stands approximately 863 metres above sea level and its base circumference is about nine kilometres. It is almost 2.5 kilometres long and 1.5 kilometres wide. Its dramatic form appears to be smooth and round from a distance, however, the sides of the rock are etched with deep gullies, caverns and overhangs caused by wind and water erosion over millions of years. After rain, water cascades from the top down the channels to the flat mulga plain below. Uluru is of great Aboriginal significance and many Dreaming stories revolve around the rock's origins and shape. Because of this important cultural link, Uluru and neighbouring Kata Tjuta were reverted to Aboriginal custodianship in 1972.

ABOVE The colours of Australia's desert are wide ranging. White dominates the dunes near Ceduna, a town which borders the Nullarbor Plain in South Australia.

LEFT The eerie Pinnacles in Western Australia lie within the Nambung National Park. It is thought that sand has completely covered these features several times during the last millennia.

OPPOSITE Sturts Stony Desert in the far east corner of South Australia is composed of gibber plains. These small flint-like stones cover thousands of square kilometres.

ABOVE *The sculpted lunettes at Mungo National Park have hidden many of the country's most important archaeological finds. When this area contained a large lake lined with lush vegetation Aborigines lived on its banks. Relics from those times are buried in the mounds.*

TOP *Palm Valley in central Northern Territory contains plants that grow nowhere else in the world. The valley is part of the Finke Gorge National Park.*

ABOVE *The pink evening light creates soothing images out of dunes at the dry Willandra Lakes.*

LEFT *Saltpans stretch across parts of the Simpson Desert. These sediments are left from an era when the region was a vast sea.*

BELOW *The almost featureless scrub desert around Maryvale in the south of the Northern Territory is a result of massive erosion of an ancient plateau. Nearby Chambers Pillar is all that remains of the original upland.*

ABOVE *Long red sand dunes are the most remembered features of the Simpson Desert. Some ridges run for hundreds of kilometres and four-wheel-drive enthusiasts take to this outback region with relish.*

FOLLOWING PAGES *In this dramatic late afternoon light, the mounds of Kata Tjuta adopt more mythical proportions. They appear almost druid-like.*

INDEX

PHOTOGRAPHIC TECHNICAL NOTES

The majority of pictures in this book were photographed with Canon EOS 1n cameras and 17–35mm
f2.8L, 28–70mm f2.8L and 70–200mm f2.8L Canon EF lenses on Fuji Velvia film, rated at 100 ISO. The
publishers would like to thank the Hanimex Corporation for their help in the supply of film stock.

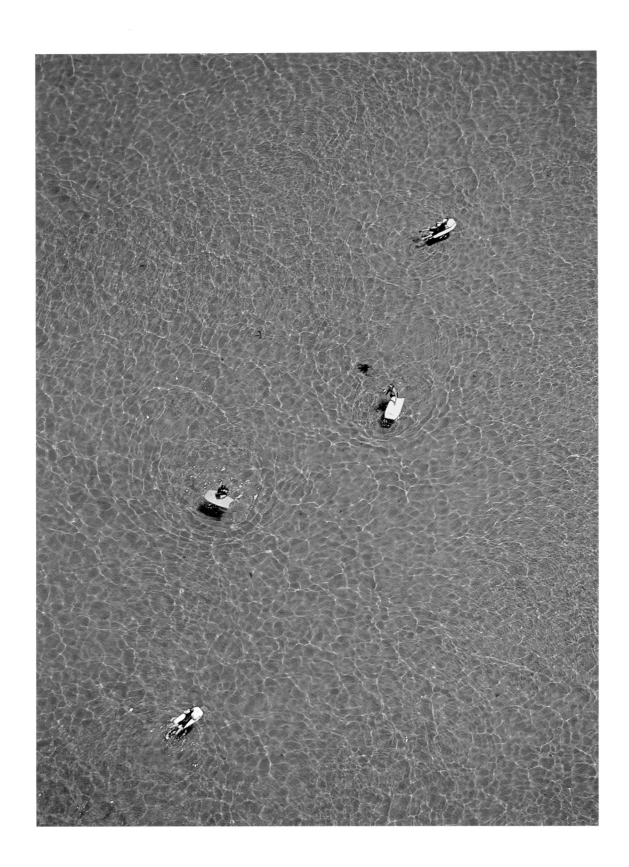